A Short Guide to Writing about Theatre

The Short Guide Series

Under the Editorship of
SYLVAN BARNET
MARCIA STUBBS

A Short Guide to Writing about Theatre

MARCIA L. FERGUSON
University of Pennsylvania

New York   Boston   San Francisco
London   Toronto   Sydney   Tokyo   Singapore   Madrid
Mexico City   Munich   Paris   Cape Town   Hong Kong   Montreal

Senior Acquisitions Editor: Katherine Meisenheimer
Marketing Manager: Thomas DeMarco
Production Manager: Savoula Amanatidis
Project Coordination, Text Design, and Electronic Page Makeup:
  GGS Book Services, Inc.
Cover Design Manager: John Callahan
Senior Manufacturing Buyer: Dennis Para
Printer and Binder: Courier Corporation—Westford
Cover Printer: Coral Graphics Services, Inc.

Cover Image: Martin Rayner and Mark Alhadeff in The Wilma Theater's 2000
production of Tom Stoppard's *The Invention of Love*. Photo credit: Permission
courtesy of The Wilma Theater. Photographer: Jim Roese.

Library of Congress Cataloging-in-Publication Data
Ferguson, Marcia L.
   A short guide to writing about theatre / Marcia L. Ferguson.
      p. cm.—(The short guide series)
   Includes bibliographical references and index.
   ISBN-13: 978-0-321-13673-2 (alk. paper)
   ISBN-10: 0-321-13673-X (alk. paper)
      1. Dramatic criticism. I. Title.

PN1707.F47 2008
808.2—dc22

                                                              2007019537

Please visit us at www.ablongman.com

ISBN-13: 978-0-321-13673-2
ISBN-10: 0-321-13673-X

   4 5 6 7 8 9 10—CRW—10 09

To Tim

Two figures in a nature of the sun,
In the sun's design of its own happiness.

Wallace Stevens

Contents

Preface

Associated mainly with the practical arts of acting, designing, and directing, theatre is sometimes overlooked as the rich academic discipline it also is. The study of theatre is an ideal way to encourage students to write because it encompasses so many literary, cultural, political, and artistic histories and movements, and so offers student writers such rich thematic possibilities, that it appeals to a range of interests and backgrounds. Without the writing skills to engage in these various ways of thinking about theatre, however, valuable classroom time is lost in teaching the mechanics of the essay, or other modes of writing that are essential to analyzing drama and theatre practice. This book was written in the hope that a guide to the basic principles of writing about theatre—both as an academic subject and as a living, practical art form—will save time and energy in all kinds of theatre classrooms.

The book's structure builds from essential, pre-writing activities (such as note taking while reading a play or watching a production, interpreting assignments, and creating an outline) to the process of writing about theatre in various modes (such as the review, the production response, the analytical essay, and the character/scene analysis), to information on research and gathering and organizing materials. The six chapters are supplemented by a glossary of theatrical terms and concepts, and an index. Special features that facilitate student use include:

- Epigraphs offering noteworthy commentary on chapter content
- Annotated sample student papers
- Sample paper topics
- Concrete suggestions for using and describing stage space and stage composition in written analysis
- Step-by-step examples of drafting and revising
- Thorough coverage of research and documentation
- Checklists for writing activities, such as taking good notes, finding paper topics, and organizing and incorporating research
- Production stills and graphics illustrating theatrical concepts and related writing techniques

The approaches introduced here are meant to be adaptable to various instructor preferences and positions—for example, it will be as useful to an English or History class studying a play or performance in an academic, literary, or historical context, as it is to an Acting, Directing, or Introduction to Theatre class working on plays as performance pieces, study projects, or generic examples. Students learn about theatre in various ways, and whether they find themselves on the floor breathing deeply in relaxation exercises in an acting class, improvising with set pieces for laboratory scenes in directing class, or taking notes in a theatre history seminar, they will at some point need to refine their thinking through written analysis. Writing critically about their intellectual, physical, and emotional connection to theatrical experience not only enhances their understanding of theatre's complexities, but also increases their pleasure in its unfolding. In the end, my hope is that this book allows all theatre students and teachers more class time to create and pursue the imaginative and intellectual pleasures of their discipline.

I am grateful to many individuals for their assistance in helping me write this book. I thank my colleagues at the University of Pennsylvania, especially Rosemary Malague, Cary Mazer, James Schlatter, Peter Whinnery, and David Fox, for generously sharing their wealth of knowledge, talent, skill, and camaraderie with me. Many people inspired me to complete this project through their own examples of scholarship, practice, or plain perseverance, including Leslie Spiro, Hildy Tow, Dana Prescott, and M. Carr Ferguson. I thank Lauren Anderson and the many editors and experts at Longman who have ushered this project through its long gestation period, and I am grateful to the many readers whose critiques were so essential to the manuscript's development: Thomas Adler, Purdue University; Darrell Anderson, University of Dayton; Cecilia Aragon, University of Wyoming; Wendy Arons, University of Notre Dame; Ann Bliss, Western Oregon University; Barbara Bray, University of Arkansas; Ken Bright, Southern Illinois University; Shane Fuller, East Texas Baptist University; Deborah Greer Currier, Western Washington University; Mac Groves, Northern Arizona University; Dr. Kristin Johnsen-Neshati, George Mason University; Shannon Miller, Temple University; Timothy Murray, Cornell University; Andrew Ryder, Seattle Pacific University; Owen W. Schaub, Butler University; James F. Wilson,

LaGuardia Community College. Sylvan Barnet's invaluable, expert guidance was generous in the extreme. Thanks to Sandy Huckleberry for her excellent graphics and her sense of adventure. My students deserve my gratitude for teaching me so much, as do my former teachers and directors (especially Daniel Gerould, Marvin Carlson, Paul Berman, Dugald MacArthur, and Blanka and Jiri Zizka) for modeling such excellence in practice and in pedagogy. I thank my wonderful parents, sisters, and entire extended family for offering me time to write and time to play, especially in the summers. My children, Cecilia, Graham, and Anna, sustain me always with their love, encouragement, antics, forbearance, and good humor. Finally, I am most truly grateful to my husband, Timothy, for his dedication to all things visual, for his excellent advice, and most especially for his joie de vivre.

Marcia L. Ferguson
University of Pennsylvania

A Short Guide to
Writing about Theatre

1

WRITING ABOUT
THEATRE

Drama is life with the dull bits cut out.
—ALFRED HITCHCOCK

WHY WRITE ABOUT THEATRE?

Theatre is all around us, describing most of our daily lives as we
play diverse roles as teachers and students, parents and children,
librarians and grocery clerks. On the first day of a college class, how
can you tell who the teacher is at first glance? Most likely, by his or
her "costume": the teacher will be more formally attired than the
students. The clothes we wear and the actions we take reflect our
character and our function in society, just as surely as costumes suit
characters we watch on stage, whether we wear business suits,
aprons, or prison garb. Although few of us regularly go to the theatre, there are countless ways in which the language of theatre
informs our lives: troublesome kids are "acting out," your academic
"performance" determines your grades, and when you die, it's "cur-
tains" for you. Peter Brook gets right to the point: "Theatre is life."

But why write about something that is a part of everyday life or
something we rarely attend? Because plays contain essential ideas,
passions, histories, and emotions that use the materials of life to lift
us to new ways of seeing, thinking, and feeling. They therefore offer
students an excellent focus for a sustained piece of writing. They are
carefully ordered around concepts, emotions, or characters that are
designed to have maximum emotional and/or intellectual impact

on the audience or reader. They come out of a specific historical moment and cultural milieu and offer rich resources for the writer seeking both personal and complex material for an essay. Perhaps you have an assignment to write a paper for a literature class and wish to write about a play, playwright, era, or dramatic movement (such as classicism, romanticism, or realism). Maybe you are studying acting, directing, dramaturgy, or design and need to write specifically about one particular aspect of (or approach to) theatrical production. Or perhaps you want to write theatre reviews for a college or local newspaper. Whatever the form, theatre is a great way to engage your personal aesthetic as well as the artistic, intellectual, political, historical, and cultural ideas and conditions affecting performance or plays.

All writing about theatre requires:

- critical perception
- evaluation, and
- careful organization.

When attending a production you will be writing about, it is a good idea to do the following:

1. *Take notes during the show, at intermission, or as soon after seeing the show as possible.* The sooner you jot down your impressions of specific scenes, effects, settings, and so on, the better, as your impressions of important details are easily and quickly forgotten.
2. *Save the theatre program* so that you will have a reference for the names of the actors, director, and designers.
3. *Note your opinions and first impressions* in a kind of free-form first draft, without the constraint of a narrow thesis topic. You will refine and organize your impressions in later drafts.

Theatre writing can be distinguished by the kind of relationship it has with the reader. The following excerpts demonstrate two ways that the sense of a reader and the writer's opinion can come together in good, persuasive theatre writing. The first example is a brief section of a review, written for readers of a local daily newspaper. Although reviews often contain an introductory paragraph giving an overview of the play's plot, notice that this reviewer assumes that the reader is already familiar with the play because it is a classic, *Hedda Gabler*, by Henrik Ibsen. The writer instead focuses on evaluating the acting, the design, and the directing.

Sample Review

Frankly, I never liked Hedda very much anyway and I've never been able to see her as a victim of society's image of women. Director Derek Shore has combined a messy phantasmagoric stage and a cast of undisciplined actors to provide a backdrop for Hedda's self-indulgence. Basically it gives an impression of churning emotional turmoil which I assume is what is intended. Hedda is interpreted with a nice combination of arrogance and self-mockery by Cynthia Collier who struts and frets very well indeed. It's a good role for a strong actress but it would be better if she were surrounded by less frippery and more stark reality. I think it must be difficult to do a tough emotional performance in the midst of farcical comedy, and Collier works hard to pull it off. Logan Fox as the ill-fated Loevborg, Sarah Kate Anderson as the pathetic Thea, Daniel Beckner as the smug Judge, and Morgan White as the much maligned Tesman all make an effort to contribute to the context of the play—but the ambiguity of the script and direction leaves them and the rest of the cast vacillating uncertainly between comedy and tragedy. Set design by Maggie Erickson can best be described as conglomerate. She has a lot of space to fill and she does it with enthusiasm. Lighting by Kelly Kumaniec is mostly dark and red. My compliments to the props master, Robyn James, who certainly collected an amazing amount of, well, stuff.[1]

Sooner or later, a reviewer offers the reader a *recommendation* about whether the production is—or is not—worth seeing. A reviewer may also want the reader to think about some of the larger artistic, political, or social issues the play raises, but that is not usually the goal of a popular review; its main distinctive feature remains its *descriptive quality* and its ability to persuade the reader. Using evidence from their experience of the production to back it

[1]Ann Bennett, "Hedda Gabler Review," *Santa Cruz Sentinel*, 23 February 2006.

up, reviewers offer their opinions of the work and argue their point. Because reviews are usually published in popular journals such as *Time* magazine or in newspapers, their style is usually more casual than the style of a critical analysis: for example, a review might use a contraction, such as "don't waste your money," or might use, as in the example just quoted, a colloquial or slang word, such as "stuff," whereas a more formal analysis normally will not.

The second example is a critical analysis about the same play, Ibsen's *Hedda Gabler*, written for readers of an academic journal:

Sample Analysis

A small but extremely telling example of Breth's symbolic imagination is established early in the play, when Tesman brings in and places prominently on the piano a detailed model Viking ship he has apparently assembled at some time in the past. This ship, which like other items of furniture drifts rather aimlessly about the room in the remaining acts, is richly suggestive. Most directly it seems perfectly suited to Tesman's character, a project requiring the patient assembling of small bits of material, to an end ultimately more decorative than useful and suggestive perhaps more of the enthusiasm of an adolescent hobby than an attitude of serious engagement with the world.

On a deeper level, however, the ship also seems to suggest something about the basic tensions of the play itself, and indeed of a theme that runs through much of Ibsen's theatre. The once mighty, free and untrammeled Viking existence has in modern times been domesticated and civilized, reduced to the seemingly harmless confines of legends, stories, and toys for children. The cost of his domestication has been very high culturally and personally, however, and constantly in Ibsen's plays, as in this one, something of that repressed vigor returns, in the excesses of a Lovborg or in the neurotic repression of a Hedda Gabler. As the detailed little Viking ship drifts about the Schaubhune stage, then, it serves as a constant visual reminder of the personal and cultural tensions that are driving Hedda, and those around her, to the final catastrophe.[2]

[2]Marvin Carlson, "Andrea Breth's *Hedda Gabler*," *Western European Stages* 7: 61–62.

The goal of this writer, Marvin Carlson, is to offer the reader an *intellectual engagement* with the production in question, based on a solid *analysis* of it. An analysis (the word literally means a breaking of something down into component pieces, the better to understand it as a whole) examines specific parts of a production, and shows how those pieces fit together to create a whole and how in turn the whole of the play relates to larger ideas, trends, and ideologies. Carlson's analytical essay argues that a relatively small element in the play, a property model Viking ship, represents larger issues and ideas: it demonstrates the symbolic approach of the director, it reveals the way Ibsen constructed Tesman's character, and, on an even larger level, it evokes the relationship of the Vikings to modern culture. He offers the reader this perspective as a way to think about how symbols were used to create certain effects in this particular production and to see the play itself in larger historical and sociological terms.

Both examples examine theatre as an art form and a living, changing entity, but they do so from different perspectives. The style of each piece demonstrates a different relationship with the reader. The review, aimed at the casual theatregoer, generally employs more casual language (the properties are "an amazing amount of, well, stuff" and the lead actress works hard to "pull it off"), and the focus is on evaluating the production so that the reader can decide whether to go to it. The critical analysis, aimed at a reader who wants a deeper understanding of the play, looks at the concepts underlying the production ("on a deeper level, however, the ship also seems to suggest something about the basic tensions of the play itself, and indeed of a theme that runs through much of Ibsen's theatre"). Further, the analysis sees the ship in profound social and historical terms ("it serves as a constant visual reminder of the personal and cultural tensions that are driving Hedda, and those around her, to the final catastrophe"). To put the matter simply, reviews usually aim chiefly at giving the reader a sense of whether he or she should see the production, whereas an analysis aims chiefly at deepening a reader's understanding of the play. While it is useful to distinguish between these two kinds of writing about theatre, the review and the critical analysis, in fact most writing about theatre is a mixture of both, partly evaluative (the essence of the review) and partly descriptive (the essence of an analysis). In all theatre writing, writers must take stands, assume positions, and organize their thoughts.

In a college class, you may be asked to write about a number of different dimensions of a play. Whether you are

- responding to or reviewing a specific playwright or production,
- analyzing an aspect of theatre history or a dramatic movement using research, or
- reviewing or analyzing a practical aspect of theatre you may be involved in yourself, such as acting, directing, or design,

your basic tools (tastes and opinions and using rhetoric, logic, and evidence to create convincing arguments) remain the same. Your own interests and enthusiasms are always key, and because theatre is such a multifaceted art form, with an incredible variety of material from which to choose, you will inevitably find subject matter to write about that inspires or compels you.

THE IMPORTANCE OF CONVERSATION

We often take the first step toward writing without knowing it, simply by talking about a topic. We enjoy discussing entertainments such as sporting events, movies, or television as a way of understanding them better, of sharing our opinions with others and hearing theirs in return. Conversations that take place after seeing a play similarly enhance our enjoyment of it. Listen to audiences streaming out of theatre doors after a show: they immediately start chatting about the pros and cons of the production they have just seen. "Wasn't the redhead awful?" "That was fabulous!" "What a waste of time." "What was your favorite part?" When they share their opinions, audiences relive their experiences and begin a process of refining and explaining their reactions. Sometimes—and this point is important—they change their minds about a production after hearing from other audience members, sometimes they convince others of the merits of their perspectives, and sometimes they simply reinforce each others' opinions. When you write or, more likely, when you reread your first draft, you may see that this or that point is not really clearly stated, maybe because it was not clearly thought out. In writing, and especially in revising, you engage in a conversation with yourself about your own ideas as a way of refining and expressing them clearly.

The imaginary exchange below is a case in point: it demonstrates that crucial link between talking and writing. The invented conversation, between two students leaving a production of Thornton Wilder's classic American play *Our Town* (see Figure 1a), and the paper that follows it show that discussing theatre is already a critical response and that such a response can be the start of a thoughtful essay.

Figure 1a. Emily and Stage Manager amidst umbrellas in the cemetary scene of the first Broadway production (in 1938) of *Our Town*.

Photo credit: Photofest, Inc.

ASHLEY: That was so interesting, the way the actors could make you see things that weren't there.

BRIAN: Oh, you mean the way they pretended to open doors, drive cars, and drink milkshakes on a bare stage? The sound effects helped.

ASHLEY: Yes, that must have required so much practice! At first I was surprised to see a stage with no props or scenery, but then I really appreciated how much it allowed me to focus on the play itself—the characters and the dialogue.

BRIAN: You're right—I loved the way I found myself believing that the invisible things were there, just because of the actors' ways of handling them. And I also liked the cemetery scene—it was interesting to see how much the actors' behavior changed when they were dead.

ASHLEY: That was the high point of the play for me. It was so sad and so surreal. But one thing kept bothering me—why could the stage manager hear and see everything that the ordinary characters couldn't? I mean, was he supposed to be dead or something? Who was he, anyway?

BRIAN: I just thought he was like an outside observer or commentator, whose purpose was to show us their lives. Another thing that intrigued me was the relationship between the kids and the grown-ups in the town. It was so formal and awkward. Was America really like that then, or was that just Wilder's imagination?

Ashley's one-page response to the production, required by her Introduction to Theatre class, takes as a starting point many of the topics discussed in this conversation and turns them into a simple but coherent response to the production. Her essay contains comments in the margins pointing out the essay's strengths, and it is followed by "questions for critique" that interrogate the effectiveness of the essay's form and content. Think about the answers to these questions, referring back to the essay as often as necessary. Familiarizing yourself with these kinds of questions will help you develop a critical engagement with theatrical writing, which will in turn help you write effectively about theatre.

Ashley Brock

Title conveys essay's main focus.

Seeing the Invisible: Thornton Wilder's *Our Town*

Opening paragraph describes production and writer's overall reaction to it.

Last night I saw the Union College Players' production of Thornton Wilder's *Our Town*. I knew nothing about this play before this production. I was dazzled by the beautiful imagery of the language and by the way the actors made me "see" props and sets that weren't there, merely by using gestures. For example, the two main characters went into an ice cream shop and drank "invisible" milkshakes. The sound design helped the audience visualize the milkshakes because you could hear the actors "slurping" through their straws when they got to the bottom of the glass. The play is about complex issues, like love and the nature of existence, but it is also about the everyday occurrences of ordinary small-town life. We see both levels of the play at work in the role of the narrator.

Writer moves smoothly from first to second paragraph, using "however" as a transitional link between them.

At first, however, I didn't understand who the stage manager was or if he was alive or dead. He spoke to the audience directly, and seemed to know everything. This bothered me until I realized that this mattered little. He was there to show us the town and the people in it, to give us the back story. His job was to show the audience what he wanted them to see and to act as a mediator of sorts between the spectators and the characters. But I think Wilder ultimately wants him to remain an ambiguous figure, so that the audience can decide for themselves about the play.

Writer identifies a major characteristic of play—ambiguity—and ties it into her opinion of the production.

Paragraph starts with strong evaluative statement, then supports it with concrete detail from specific scene.

My favorite moment in the play was the cemetery scene. The young housewife who had just died took a seat among the other dead people from the town, who were all sitting in neat rows, just as their tombstones were laid out. The lighting was low, and the mourners all held black umbrellas, and this created an eerie atmosphere. The dialogue showed us that the others were all patiently waiting (it's not clear what they're waiting for, only that they're waiting) but that the "newcomer" was more anxious than the rest of the dead. She wasn't used to being dead yet. When her new husband came to the grave and

Concluding sentence summarizes and evaluates.

cried, the audience cried along with him, but the young wife and the other dead were hardly disturbed at all. The excellent acting and the play itself showed that, although the living and the dead are connected within the circle of life, they are also permanently separated from one another.

Questions for Critique

1. Is the essay clearly organized? Does it have a thesis topic? If so, does it move logically from a thesis topic to a related conclusion?
2. Does this response give a sense of what it was like to be in the audience?
3. Does the essay incorporate the writer's personal point of view on the material?

Although it is not an extremely complex response to the play (it does not, for example, demonstrate knowledge of the play in the larger terms of the playwright's career, of its initial critical reception, or of its place in the canon of American drama), Ashley's essay does accomplish the major goals set out in these questions for critique. It is generally well organized and moves logically from an initial thesis ("the play is about complex issues, like love and the nature of existence, but it is also about the everyday occurrences of ordinary small-town life") to a related conclusion ("the excellent acting and the play itself showed that, although the living and the dead are connected within the circle of life, they are also permanently separated from each other"). It gives the reader a sense of what it was like to be in the audience ("I was dazzled by the beautiful imagery of the language ... the audience cried along with him"), and it incorporates Ashley's personal point of view on the material ("At first I didn't understand who the stage manager was").

The essay has potential, but it could be improved by

- a more complex argument (one, for example, that takes into account other plays by the playwright or the play's production history),
- the use of more detail in support of that argument (especially regarding the specific elements of the production), and

- the use of sources (either from the play's text or from secondary materials) to corroborate and substantiate the writer's statements regarding the play.

Still, Ashley's relatively limited experience with and knowledge of theatre has not prevented her from writing a generally thoughtful, well-organized essay about *Our Town*.

Talking about the play was a good starting place for Ashley's essay. Ashley and Brian were in basic agreement about their reaction to the play, but they had some different specific concerns and questions about it. Talking with one another about those concerns helped clarify their own positions. It gave them a good starting point as they considered what to write for their assignment. Ashley's paper was built on many of the comments and questions that came into their conversation just after the performance. It shows that even a person with no previous exposure to theatre can write about his or her own reactions and engage the fundamental idea of a play in interesting ways.

THE IMPORTANCE OF THE AUDIENCE

Writing about live theatre often also means writing about audiences. The play you watch will address you, the viewer, as if you were in dialogue with it. Spectators are one of the most important elements of the theatre: it simply doesn't exist without them. Milly Barranger put it this way: "The three basic components of theatre are the actor, the space, and the audience." In many theatrical traditions, reaching all the way from classical Greek and Roman plays to current plays, characters address the audience directly (a practice referred to as "direct address"), introducing them to the situation, asking them to keep secrets, to sympathize with a particular character, or even to overlook a character's flaws. For example, Shakespeare's *Romeo and Juliet* begins with a performer speaking directly to the audience, summarizing the plot:

> Two households, both alike in dignity,
> In fair Verona, where we lay our scene,
> From ancient grudge break to new mutiny,
> Where civil blood makes civil hands unclean.
> From forth the fatal loins of these two foes
> A pair of star-cross'd lovers take their life;

> Whose misadventur'd piteous overthrows
> Doth with their death bury their parents' strife.[3]

The audience thus immediately discovers some very important things about the play and the main characters. By addressing the audience directly, the character (and the playwright) accomplishes many things: putting us at our ease, capturing our attention, and giving us a "superior awareness" of the situation so that we can enjoy watching the characters discover what we already know. In another example of direct address, Tom, in Tennessee Williams's *The Glass Menagerie*, begins the play by telling the audience that what they are about to see is the truth:

> Yes, I have tricks in my pocket, I have things up my sleeve. But I am the opposite of a stage magician. He gives you illusion that has the appearance of truth. I give you truth in the pleasant disguise of illusion.[4]

Here Tom identifies himself as a narrator, whose point of view on the action will largely control the audience's perception of the play. The use of the "direct address" is just one example among many techniques that engage viewers as an integral part of theatre. Whatever the nature of the address of the play, however, this reciprocity between watcher and performer is significantly echoed in the relationship between the reader and the writer about theatre.

Writing about theatre requires the articulation of a personal perspective on the play so that the reader may vicariously experience either (1) being a spectator or (2) being a reader of the play or performance under discussion. It is important to note that there is a difference in how one writes about a play as a text versus a play as a performance:

- When writing about a play as text, the writer tends to pay attention to verbal elements, such as the rhetorical devices the playwright uses.
- When writing about a play as a performance, the writer must pay attention to—in addition to the text—the

---

[3]William Shakespeare, *Romeo and Juliet*, in *The Globe Illustrated Shakespeare*, ed. Howard Staunton (New York: Crown Publishers, 1983), 158.

[4]Tennessee Williams, *The Glass Menagerie*, in *Types of Drama: Plays and Essays*, 7th ed., Sylvan Barnet et al. (New York: Longman, 1997), 620.

audience and the specific elements of the production (i.e., the acting, set design, sound, and so on).

The best writing about theatre is a triangle: a vibrant, three-way engagement between the writer, the play/performance, and the reader. This is equally true whether the writer engages the subject of theatre as a live performance or as a piece of literature.

The following essays, written by students in the same class, demonstrate two very different "conversations" with the same play. Both students saw a production of Ibsen's *A Doll's House* (see Figure 1b) and were given the same assignment: a one-page response to the question, "Should *A Doll's House* Be Performed Today?" The essays are followed by the same "questions for critique" for you to think about after you have read them, with an

Figure 1b. Liv Ullman as Nora and Sam Waterston as Torvald in the 1975 Lincoln Center production of *A Doll's House.*

Photo credit: Photofest, Inc.

additional question concerning the writer's relationship to the reader. Again, try to answer them for yourself, referring back to the essays as you think about them. If you develop the capacity to recognize what is good and bad in writing about theatre, you are well on your way to good theatre writing yourself.

Hildy Cook

Ibsen's *A Doll's House*: A Timely Reminder to Feminists

Ibsen's *A Doll's House* depicts a marriage that was most likely the norm for the era in which Ibsen wrote it: the husband worked, the wife stayed at home with the children, and a significant power gap existed between them. The genius of Ibsen's play was to show how the desire to maintain the appearance of a traditional marriage ultimately destroyed it because that desire rendered any honesty between the partners impossible. The negative influence of tradition-bound roles within a marriage is demonstrated by the play's plot. *A Doll's House* should be performed today because many of the same issues that Ibsen exposes in his play continue to haunt American culture many years later. The tragic honesty of the play's plot and the sympathy Ibsen creates in the audience for Nora make this play an important reminder of how things once were between the sexes and, to a certain extent, how they still are. *A Doll's House* serves as a warning to a contemporary audience, implying that women might again be in Nora's position, if we are not careful and conscientious.

Young American women of today grow up thinking that they can accomplish anything a man can accomplish. They falsely believe that our society protects their rights to equality in school, in the workplace, and at home. Unfortunately, statistics show us that this is not the case. For example, the number of women who must drop out of the workforce to care for young children, elderly parents, or other family members is at least twice that of men. Furthermore, even if they do find sustained employment, women often hit a "glass ceiling" in the workplace, which prevents them from reaching the highest positions of power in corporations, law firms, and elsewhere. Women still make less money than men, doing the same job for less pay. In a concrete example of those same realities in Ibsen's lifetime and milieu, Nora's economic situation is desperate: she is being blackmailed for the repayment of a loan she took out to save her husband's life without his knowing it. The play shows that she is in fact a very able businesswoman but that she must pretend to be a feckless and profligate young woman in front of her husband so he won't suspect the truth. We can see this charade when she tells him, "You haven't any idea how many expenses we skylarks and squirrels have, Torvald" (7).[5] While he scolds her for buying candy, she is actually saving every penny and taking in sewing to make payments on the loan.

The young women in the audience that I sat with seemed very empathetic to Nora and her desperate situation. When Torvald, her husband, discovers the truth towards the end of the play, he reacts by condemning her: "miserable creature—what have you done?" (80). Several women in the audience gasped at this point. If Nora's situation can still evoke that kind of response, it is because sexism, domination, and inequity still exist in marriages. Otherwise, women would most likely perceive Nora as an anachronism, a relic of a different age, strange and incomprehensible. But instead too many of us recognize Nora because we have witnessed contemporary women in similar circumstances.

Therefore, it is especially critical for young audiences to watch *A Doll's House*. If we choose to see Ibsen's play as a relic of history, then we become complacent to dangerous realities within our own society. Ibsen's play is not only a crucial work of art, it is also a work of enduring sociological significance.

Larry Stillwell

Marriage and Talk: Powers of Communication in Ibsen's
A Doll's House

Ibsen's *A Doll's House* reveals that communication is the key to any successful partnership. Without it, Torvald is permitted to believe in a fantasy marriage that never existed in the first place. This play is frequently cited as a kind of feminist rallying cry

---

[5]All page references given parenthetically within the essay refer to Henrik Ibsen, *A Doll's House*, in *Eleven Plays of Henrik Ibsen* (New York: Penguin, 1943).

against the constraints of marriage, but I believe it is really the story of what can happen when the lines of communication break down. Whether in war or marriage, clear communication leads the way to victory.

Torvald is often cited as the male chauvinist antihero of Nora's story. It is true that Torvald treats Nora with condescension, that he is often arrogant and unappreciative of her. Yet it should also be said that Torvald is a product of his time and place and that he was taught to treat women like dolls, not only by his own family but also by Nora's father. Nora herself cultivates Torvald's perception of her as a doll or child, literally fluttering around the stage in his presence, dancing, eating candies, and wrapping presents for the children. She never shows him the side of herself that the audience is privileged to see, the side that is a canny businesswoman. Instead, she communicates nothing of this to Torvald, preferring to live up to his notion of what a wife should be. If she had the courage to communicate the real state of things in their household, the plot would obviously have unfolded differently. In fact, I don't even know that the play would have been written at all!

While the blackmail plot holds great dramatic tension within it, I can't help hoping for a happier ending from Ibsen. After all, isn't it quite possible that a man like Torvald could react the way Nora had hoped he would when he found out, with adoration and appreciation rather than shame and anger? Perhaps Ibsen, never at home in his home country, was working out some of his anger at his countrymen in his depiction of Torvald. In my experience, while open communication can initially cause some pain, it ultimately is the road to honest and open negotiations, in a relationship or in a business. The critics never hold Nora at fault for failing to communicate with her husband, for her lack of honesty, for living a lie to his detriment. If she had done so from the very beginning, Torvald might have had the chance to get used to the idea of her borrowing money for his health, and he might have been reconciled to it.

What we are left with, however, is a portrait of a marriage gone sour before it can even begin. A true marriage is a meeting of two individuals' minds. Nora and Torvald never openly communicate with one another, and although Torvald participates in this problem, he does not cause it alone. Their marriage is a travesty of a true marriage, which calls for open minds and hearts. Let us hope that, in the future, critics will recognize that it is not one individual or one gender that is at fault in this tragic drama but that lack of communication is the true evil in this play.

Questions for Critique

1. Is the essay clearly organized? Does it offer a thesis topic, and, if so, does it move logically from the thesis topic to a related conclusion?
2. Does this response give a sense of what it was like to be in the audience?
3. Does the essay incorporate the writer's personal point of view on the material?
4. Does the essay address the reader in a meaningful way?

Although neither essay is the work of a professional writer, the first in several ways is more successful in its execution. Because it is more clearly organized, its argument is easier to follow. Notice, for instance, that

- the first writer guides the reader by using helpful transitions such as "therefore," "furthermore," and "in a concrete example";
- some brief quotations from the play support the writer's generalizations;
- the writer uses exactly the right words (e.g., she speaks of Nora's situation as "desperate," a more accurate word than "horrifying" or "uncomfortable"); and
- each paragraph develops one idea.

In the first paragraph, for instance, the idea essentially is that Ibsen's play still has meaning in today's society because society is still plagued by sexist traditions. This idea is developed by the addition of concrete details: "the negative influence of tradition-bound roles within a marriage is demonstrated by the play's plot." In the second paragraph the idea essentially is that sexism has dire consequences and promotes dishonesty. This idea is developed both by details ("Nora's economic situation is desperate" and "she must pretend to be a feckless and profligate young woman in front of her husband") and by a few phrases quoted from the play. Finally, this writer uses specific examples from outside the play to support her thesis; for example, she relates her discussion of the "'glass ceiling' in the workplace" and traditional expectations of women as caregivers to Nora's plight.

The second writer relies more heavily on his opinions, and his logic is at times confusing. He employs generalized and vague examples without concrete details to support them, such as "In my experience, . . . open communication . . . is the road to honest and open relationships." No transitional words help guide the reader through the argument. His essay suffers from a less coherent structure; it seems likely that he spent little time thinking about his argument before he began writing. Ultimately, it is not certain if the second essay truly addresses the assignment. While the student believes that a lack of communication is the real problem in the play, he does not demonstrate why it should or should not be performed. The first writer clearly answers this question, asserting that Ibsen's work is relevant today because gender discrimination is an enduring social problem.

These very different reactions to the same production tell us that the difference of opinion resides within the writers themselves and in the way that they responded to the material. One of the interesting things about writing about theatre as a performance is that it allows us to talk about a *group* experience from the perspective of a very *individualistic* point of view. Theatre is a meeting place where a variety of opinions and tastes can come together and experience the same play at the same time, in the same room, and elicit very different responses. This "liveness" of theatre distinguishes it from many other forms of contemporary media. The technological revolution of the late twentieth century offers us many wonderful things, but most of them are available only at a remove: on a computer, in a movie, or on a television screen.

Theatre is one of the few remaining art forms that brings artists and audiences together for an event they experience at the same time, in the same place. When you write about theatre, you are also writing about the many other people (artists and audiences) who participated in your personal experience of it simply by being a part of it. In the words of Edgar Allan Poe, "One half the pleasure experienced at a theatre arises from the spectator's sympathy with the rest of the audience, and, especially, from his belief in their sympathy with him." If a play makes us sad, if it makes us laugh uproariously, or if it's an embarrassing failure, our feelings about it are shared with other audience members, as they are with the performers themselves.

TASTES AND OPINIONS

Obviously, our personal tastes will greatly affect our opinion of a play. Knowing the difference between personal tastes ("Somehow, I just don't like historical plays") and well-founded opinions ("Shakespeare's *Julius Caesar* is widely viewed as a classic") allows us to build convincing arguments, which we need to do in order to persuade the reader that our point of view is legitimate. Tastes are individual ("I prefer vanilla to chocolate") and often have more to do with our personal experience than with objective value. Opinions, on the other hand, can be formed and substantiated and can change with changing circumstances.

As mentioned before, talking about or thinking through your reaction to a performance is a key preliminary step to forming an opinion, and casual conversations after seeing a play can often reveal what you really think about something or, at the very least, your initial response to it. Articulating your response to a play is a process whereby opinions become (ideally convincing) arguments. We can easily imagine, for example, the following conversation between two friends leaving the theatre after seeing a production of August Wilson's *Fences* (see Figure 1c):

> ABBY: I just didn't get it. That play was so unrealistic. Why did Rose stay with Troy when he was unfaithful to her? I couldn't believe that Rose would raise Troy's baby from his mistress at the end. I don't think anyone would really do that. And it was so mean of him not to let Cory play football—wouldn't a father be proud of a son who got recruited like that? And I guess I didn't like all that yelling and anger; there should have been more humor in the play.
>
> SARAH: I see what you mean, but I actually really liked the play. Troy wasn't perfect, but he really did love Rose and all his family. He didn't want Cory to play football because he didn't want to see him get hurt. And I thought it was so moving when Rose decided to take in his baby. She also wasn't perfect—she was a gambler.
>
> ABBY: I guess you're right. It's just that I didn't like the character of Troy at all, and he was supposed to be the main

Figure 1c. James Earl Jones as Troy Maxon and Lynne Thigpen as Rose Maxon in the 1988 Broadway production of *Fences*.

Photo credit: Photofest, Inc.

> protagonist, so it was really hard for me to like the whole play. Maybe a different actor could have been more sympathetic.
>
> SARAH: But I also really liked the symbolism in the play. I thought it got the point across, that people were fenced in, fenced off from society, and put up their own fences to protect themselves, for better or worse.

Once again, within this casual conversation are the seeds of two opinions—and therefore two different essays—on this particular production of the play. Abby's objections are partly based on her inability to "believe in" the play's plot and on her basic preference for lighter theatre ("there should have been more humor in the play"), but she also has some points to make about the casting and lack of clarity in the production, which, if she thought it through and supplied supporting detail, could very well send her on her way toward an effective critique. Sarah has some clear ideas about why she liked the production despite what she admits are some drawbacks. If she were to align her thoughts coherently and, again, supply more concrete detail about the production, she could marshal a convincing argument in the production's favor. Both approaches are legitimate *opinions*, which can then be marshaled into effective, convincing arguments. To transform opinion into argument, a writer needs the following:

- Evidence or facts: citing specific lines, scenes, design details, and so on that support your idea
- Logic: linking evidence to conclusions in a cause-and-effect manner
- Rhetoric: using language that is both clear and convincing

The above conversation starts us on the road to some important distinctions regarding our reactions to plays. *Taste* might incline us to like or dislike something, without subjecting that inclination to any hard, critical thinking. It's a basic orientation, not a full-fledged idea. *Opinions*, on the other hand, can be formed and can change with changing circumstances and experiences. For example, Abby thought the play was unrealistic and the main character unsympathetic. Sarah thought the play was enlightening and moving. Either opinion can be valid, as long as the *evidence* supporting it is well chosen, is *logically* organized, and is *rhetorically* convincing. Your tastes and opinions will be key to finding your voice as a writer and to finding topics that interest you, which, in turn, lead to persuasive, convincing, and engaging arguments about theatre.

YOUR AUDIENCE

As we have seen, an essay is in dialogue with its reader. Notice the importance of *your* own audience as you write the essay. There is a vast difference between an essay written for an audience of subscribers to a school newspaper, for example, and one written for a college class, whose members presumably share a relatively detailed acquaintance with the specific issues and arguments that pertain to your thesis. Your sense of your audience will help you establish the appropriate *tone* of your essay. A relatively formal tone will be required in an essay written for a course; do not use slang, contractions, or informal modes of address. The first- and second-person modes, "I" and "you," should be used sparingly, if at all, in a formal essay. It is generally acceptable, for example, for a writer to use the first person when introducing or concluding an argument: "In this essay I will examine the way in which the symbol of the fence illustrates Troy Maxon's experience in an oppressive society." The first person should not be used in this kind of essay, however, to express the writer's unexamined feelings because this does not clarify the argument or help guide the reader. Here is an example of an unacceptable use of the first person (and also a colloquial tone) in a formal essay: "I can't stand family dramas like *Fences*, and I thought the play was way too serious."

A review for a popular press, on the other hand, can have a relatively casual tone; slang, the use of the first-person mode, and other informal ways of writing may be used, as long as the writing is still clear. For example, the tone and language of the following example would be acceptable in a popular review: "Run, don't walk, to the City Players production of *The Pajama Game*! I laughed myself silly, and you will, too." In both formal and informal writing, an awareness of your audience and of your limits in terms of pages assigned will help you develop your argument and establish your tone.

An awareness of the reader/audience is as important to the writer *about* theatre as it is to the writer *of* theatre. Writing is about the interpretation of meaning, and good writing helps persuade your reader of the merit of your interpretation. What distinguishes good and bad interpretations and good and bad writing is sustained, convincing *argument*. Our next task is to discover and implement the steps to creating good arguments—and therefore good writing—about theatre.

✔ A Checklist for Writing Reviews and Analyses

❑ Is the title informative and engaging?

❑ Do I describe the play or production (especially if it is a new play or interpretation)?

❑ Is there a cohesive topic or main focus?

❑ Does the essay have a "flow"; that is, do the paragraphs build logically one from another, and is there a related introduction and a conclusion?

❑ Have I made my opinion into a sound, persuasive evaluation or argument?

❑ Do I use concrete details (evidence) to support my broad statements?

❑ Have I used the appropriate tone, style, and language for the assignment?

2

PREPARING TO WRITE AND WRITING THE ESSAY

By writing you learn to write.
—Latin Proverb

This chapter, containing concise guidelines for writing a convincing essay on theatre, outlines simple steps to take before you even turn on your computer. These are equally useful whether you are writing about a play you have read or about a performance you have watched. The first section concerns things to do *before* you write, which we'll call "prewriting." They are essential because they help make the process of writing, which is inherently messy and confused at the start, logical, systematic, and even personally meaningful since part of prewriting involves deciding on your own relationship to the theatre you watch or read. The second section contains the mechanics of writing the essay, with topics such as finding and developing a thesis statement, developing an outline, building a convincing argument through the body paragraphs, and structuring a tight conclusion.

PREWRITING: INTERPRETING THE ASSIGNMENT

The first step in prewriting is to examine and understand your assignment. Two main kinds of theatre essays are assigned in college courses: those with specific topics and those without them.

Each type of essay asks something different of you in your initial approach to the assignment. Following are approaches to the two basic types of assigned essay topics.

Specific Paper Topics

In the case of assignments with specific topics, it is impossible to overstress the importance of *reading your assignment carefully*. It is easy to misread an essay topic or question, and although you may write a good essay, if you have misinterpreted the original assignment, you may well receive a failing grade or have to write it all over again. *Read it carefully* and make sure you understand what is being asked. For example, what is being asked of you in the following assigned topic?

Sample Specific Paper Topic

- George Bernard Shaw and Bertolt Brecht wrote plays that were intended to *reflect* and *affect* society in some way. Choose one play by each author and compare and contrast their socialist content.

After reading the assignment carefully and perhaps discussing it with some classmates, you can ascertain exactly what you are being asked to do: (1) choose one play from each author, (2) choose plays that specifically engage the issue at hand ("reflect/affect society"), and (3) develop an argument based on a comparison of the two. Writing down *exactly what is asked for* is a good practice. If you are tempted to include more than one play by one of the authors, for example, or to stray from the subject assigned, you can refer to your own interpretation of the assignment to get back on track. Notice that this breakdown of the assignment also contains the seeds of an outline: within the body of the essay, you might well follow a structure similar to the one you have evolved in your careful reading of the assignment. That is, you might well begin your paper by naming and briefly describing the plays chosen for the paper (section 1), then explain how they engage the issue (section 2), and then begin your comparison of them (section 3).

Sample Nonspecific Paper Topics

On the other hand, many assignments require the student to come up with a topic, and this freedom can be intimidating and burdensome. Deciding on your own topic is also an excellent exercise, for the practice forces you to develop your own tastes, opinions, and imagination. A liberal arts education is, after all, intended to prepare you to bring your own powers of interpretation to any experience you encounter. In the following example of a nonspecific paper topic, what is being asked of you?

- Identify and discuss a major theme in the play of your choice.

Again, writing down *exactly what is asked for* is a good idea, although here the task is far simpler than in the earlier example: you must choose a *play*, decide on a major *theme* in it, and *discuss* it. For instance, you might choose Lorraine Hansberry's *A Raisin in the Sun*, and you might decide that the major theme of this play is the *effect of racism on family relationships*. Your discussion will include *examples from the text that identify the theme*. Or, in another example, you might choose *Macbeth* and decide that a major theme of this play is the *relationship of power and ambition*. Your discussion may include an *examination of characters* who are ambitious and seek power. In both examples, simply writing exactly what is asked for in the assignment—that is, the name of the play, a major theme, and at least one way to discuss it—is a good way to start the writing process.

However, within that simplicity is the burden of choice: Which play (and which theme) best suits your purposes? How and in what context will you discuss it? Will you watch and respond to a live performance, or will you focus only on an analysis of the play as a text? As always, it is best to rely on your own tastes and enthusiasm. Is there a play, playwright, or current production that excites you in some way? Or, conversely, is there a topic or subject matter that particularly draws your attention? Once you have chosen your play, the danger of this open-ended assignment is that it is entirely without limits or structure. In this case, the burden is on you to set your *own* limits rather than relying on the assignment to do it for you. A wide-open, meandering discussion of a theme, without a structured thesis, argument, and conclusion, will not say anything concrete and thus will not be successful. You will have fulfilled the dictates of this nonspecific assignment only when you have developed a clear thesis statement, an argument backed by convincing evidence, and a conclusion that is rhetorically sound. Developing a focus is your first step.

DETERMINING SCOPE AND TONE

It is critical to determine the scope and tone of your paper before you begin the writing process. On the one hand, you want an argument that can be developed broadly enough to be of interest to your reader but not so broad that it ends up saying nothing. For example, the topic "Tragic Death in *Hamlet*" is so broad that it probably will not offer the reader any new or intriguing information about that play. On the other hand, you do not want a topic so small and precise that it is in the end trivial and unimportant. As always, asking the right questions will help you determine what *scope* your paper will have and what *tone* will be appropriate for the essay. As mentioned in chapter 1, the tone has to do with your audience, your readers. Knowing who you are writing for helps develop your focus because it forces you to be specific about what you are aiming to do with your writing. Are you evaluating the play for someone with no knowledge of the subject? Then your focus may well be on describing it so that your reader may be persuaded of your own conclusions about it. Are you analyzing the play for someone who already knows something about it? Then your focus may be on deepening the reader's understanding of the play or production you are discussing. In general, when writing a college paper, think of writing for your peers and classmates—readers with some previous understanding of the subject matter. They may well have read or seen the play and know some general information on the author, dramatic movement, or the general history of your subject matter, but they are not experts and will desire more information about it.

Scope

How many pages are assigned? You will not want to add an in-depth biography of a playwright, for example, if your paper is limited to three pages. With short assignments, such as two or three pages, you must make every word count toward your central argument, and each sentence must in some way build up or contribute to the proof of your contention. On the other hand, if you have a long assignment—say more than ten pages—you can afford a broader scope and can incorporate more diverse elements into your argument, such as pertinent details of the playwright's life.

Tone

For whom are you writing the paper? A class that has been studying *Hamlet* will not need to be told the plot, nor will you need to discuss Shakespeare's importance to literature; you can assume that your readers are familiar with both topics. Instead, you can get straight to the task of stating your thesis and proving your argument. On the other hand, if you are reviewing a new play that very few people have seen, then it may be necessary to contextualize the production with some background information about the playwright, plays that she or he has written before, or any external information (such as politics or history) that may be specifically pertinent to the play (and/or to your review of it). For example, a relatively little-known South African playwright who is writing about some personally experienced racial incident should be noted as such, especially if it has bearing on the construction (by the author) and reception (by the audience) of the play.

COMING PREPARED TO A PLAY

After you have developed an understanding of the assignment, the next step is to specifically prepare yourself for the play, whether you will be seeing a production or reading the text. It is impossible to write an essay about every aspect of a play or production; such an essay would run to hundreds of pages and probably would be boring to read. If you are asked to come up with a paper topic for a theatre class, you must find one specific focus out of a myriad of plays or productions to choose from, and, confronted with innumerable choices, ironically students are sometimes left with the feeling that they have "nothing to write about." Three easy questions can help:

- What are your interests?
- What do you know about the play, playwright, or production?
- What are your expectations?

These questions prepare you to take fruitful notes on the production (if you are watching it) or play (if you are reading it) by deciding on certain things to watch for, facilitating the topic-finding process. In short, these questions will help you find an idea for your essay that will sustain your (and your reader's) enthusiasm. Taking some time to decide on a focus beforehand can greatly reduce the amount of time spent searching for a "way into" a play or production.

Question 1: What Are Your Interests?

Give yourself a basic orientation before you attend the production or read the play. Decide what your *own* interests are and watch for elements in the play or production that have to do with them. Observe them and try to develop an opinion about them as you read or watch. For example, do you know a lot about economics or mathematics?

- Consider the role of finances in *A Doll's House*. Nora's first stage direction is to open her purse and tip the porter. Her first dialogue with Torvald concerns money. How do finances reveal important aspects of their relationship? Or, in another example,
- Explore the funding of a particular theatre's season or even of just one of its productions. How do ticket sales factor into their choice of plays? How do finances intersect with their artistic choices? Say you are frequently more interested in set, costume, or lighting design or other production effects than in plot. Again, observing these elements could lead you to a fruitful focus for your essay. For instance:

  > Consider the lighting design in *The Glass Menagerie*. The first stage direction concerning lighting says that the audience is "faced with the dark, grim rear wall of the Wingfield tenement." In Tom's first speech, he says "Being a memory play, it is dimly lighted . . ." Or, in another instance,

  > Consider the sound effects in Arthur Miller's *Death of a Salesman*, ranging from flute music to banging on the door. How do these effects contribute to the overall effect of the play?

Sample Demonstration of the Question at Work In this example, a student asked herself *what she was interested in* and decided that she was interested in *acting*. Bearing that in mind, she decided to read a play and observe a production with particular attention to the acting of the roles. Arthur Miller's *Death of a Salesman* happened to be playing on campus, so she chose that play as her subject. She first read the play and took notes on it with regard to acting. An excerpt of her notes on reading the play looked like this:

> Actor playing Willy must be vulnerable looking, not too tall or strong
>
> Relationship between Biff and Happy important—actors must be able to create believable brotherly bond
>
> How should actors play nonrealistic scenes?

She then attended the performance of the play on campus. Her notes on the production looked like this:

> Actor playing Willy—nervous tic. Intentional or stage fright?
>
> Actress playing Linda strong, believable—you can see her concern for Willy just from her body posture
>
> Actor playing Biff has high voice, whiny/annoying; actor playing Hap, soft voice, can't hear everything he says—don't seem like brothers
>
> All acting gets stylized when Willy enters his memories/nonrealistic scenes—director's choice?

These notes pointed her in several interesting directions. She decided on two possible approaches to her paper, both stemming from her notes about acting. One was about the acting of the nonrealistic scenes in the play (she believed that the stylized acting she saw in the live production ultimately weakened the play), and the other concerned the casting choices made in the performance of the play she had attended (she felt that the actors playing Willy, Biff, and Happy had all been miscast). In either case, thinking about the play in terms of her own interest sped up the process of finding a topic and quickly helped her formulate a meaningful thesis about the casting and acting of the play.

Question 2: What Do You Know about the Play, Playwright, or Production?

This question represents another approach to preparing to take fruitful notes. Thinking about elements of the play or production you already know about or are curious about is a helpful way of organizing your thinking. After all, as Samuel Johnson said, "All knowledge is of itself of some value. There is nothing so minute or inconsiderable that I would not rather know it than not." Having some particular question in mind about the material as you watch or read can frequently lead you to a topic for your paper.

Sample Demonstration of the Question at Work A student assigned to write a paper for a Shakespeare course asks himself *what he already knows about it*. The only Shakespeare plays he had seen were two productions of *A Midsummer Night's Dream*, one a high school production, and the other an avant-garde production he watched on videotape for the class. The forest in the high school production consisted of trees and flowers made of painted plywood filling the stage, whereas in the avant-garde production abstract Chinese screens and scarves created the magical environment. The student was interested in the way in which the forest (where the young lovers escape from the adult word) was differently depicted in the two productions he had already seen. Since he already knew something about *A Midsummer Night's Dream* and since what he knew about it centered on design, he decided to focus on this play and its design in performance. His first step was to take notes about design issues as he read the play. The question he posed to himself was, "What are the design requirements for the forest in this play?" An excerpt from his notes on the play look like this:

> Forest needs places for Puck to hide, space for humans to sleep and get "lost" in
>
> Colors—must have shadow/light to trick humans
>
> Visibility and invisibility important
>
> Differences between court and forest must be strong
>
> Puck and fairies—how magical should they be?

His notes suggested several interesting possible directions for his paper topic, and he decided to do a little research into the history of the design of the forest in previous productions. Picking up the textbook used in the course (Oscar Brockett's *History of the Theatre*), he simply looked up the play title in the index. There he discovered that Herbert Beerbohm Tree's 1900 production of *A Midsummer Night's Dream* was famous because it "featured live rabbits and a carpet of grass with flowers that could be plucked." As he researched and read reviews of that production, he looked for commentary on the design and execution of the forest's setting, taking notes on those aspects he felt were especially rich in meaning. An excerpt of his notes on his research looks like this:

> *Director Tree made forest as "real" as possible—was Puck realistic too?*
>
> *Puck—used light and shadow to make magic*
>
> *Realism used in design of fantasy world—ironic*

These notes led the student ever closer to a good, useful topic. He narrowed it down to two possibilities. This first was an examination of how this particular "magical" play ironically inspired Tree's interest in a realistic design (making images as realistic as possible, i.e., using live animals and real grass). The other was an evaluation of how Tree's fascination with design and particular special effects (such as the use of onstage animals) shaped his interpretation of specific language and imagery. The student's focus was not on Shakespeare's play itself but rather on how the play inspired a famous director and how its themes were expressed through Tree's sets. His decision to look at what he already knew about *A Midsummer Night's Dream* led him to take constructive notes, which in turn led him to his topic.

Question 3: What Are Your Expectations?

Answering this question before you attend a production or read a play can help you by forcing you to organize your thoughts into "before" and "after" categories. Perhaps you have heard or read something about the play, or your professor has mentioned something in class about the kind of work the theatre, director, or acting troupe has done previously. Maybe you have seen the film version of the play in question. Or perhaps even something as seemingly simple as the play's title has filled you with certain expectations ("With a title like *Red Scare on Sunset*, I was expecting a gangster story, not a satire of 1950s melodramas performed by actors in drag"). Noting down your expectations *before* you see or read the play can give you a useful jumping-off point and can help give your notes some organization. Whether your expectations are met, exceeded, or, on the contrary, disappointed, questioning why something did or did not live up to your expectations can be a fruitful way to frame your inquiry.

Sample Demonstration of the Question at Work A student in an Introduction to Theatre class had an opportunity to see a performance of a Kabuki troupe visiting his college campus. Because he had read about this subject in a Japanese history class and had seen short clips of various Kabuki performances, he knew that Kabuki theatre was a traditional and popular form of Japanese theatre featuring elaborate, colorful costumes, dynamic movement, and onstage musicians. His paper assignment was to write on any aspect of performance. He decided to use the Kabuki performance as the focus of this paper. Asking himself what his expectations were, he took a few minutes before going to the performance to jot down an answer. An excerpt from these notes about what he expected to see looks like this:

Lots of physicality, dance and showmanship

Colorful costumes

Musical accompaniment

Performer's strength and vitality highlighted

He decided to look for these qualities when taking notes at the performance. However, the Kabuki story he saw was about a frail female character who endures suffering and loss. Since women do not traditionally act in Kabuki, the women's roles were all played by men. Instead of the strength and physicality he expected, there was a lot of standing still and striking of delicate poses. The actors' goals were evidently to demonstrate how well they could play women, not to show off their male physicality. His notes show his initial confusion:

Male actor playing female character—why?

Delicate dance movements with fan

No jumping or show of strength?

Music very slow—actor holds pose for long time

The difference between his expectations and the reality of the performance intrigued this student. His notes led him in several directions, but he narrowed it down to two: he would write either about the *onnagata* (male actors specializing in portraying female characters) or about the use of opposite poles of movement in Kabuki theatre: stillness and dynamism. In either case, he decided to frame his essay with the difference between his expectations (based on what he read of it) and the reality of watching live Kabuki theatre.

Spending a bit of time preparing before you examine the text or production is the most timesaving preliminary step you can take when it comes to writing about almost any topic. Whether you use

- your own interests;
- your previous knowledge of the play, playwright, production, or topic; or
- your expectations of the play or performance,

organizing your perceptions according to these questions helps prepare you to take effective notes.

✔ *A Checklist for Finding Paper Topics*

❑ Have you read specific paper assignments carefully (at least two or three times)?

❑ Have you written down exactly what is asked for?

❑ For nonspecific paper assignments, have you chosen a play, playwright, or theme that interests you?

❑ For both specific and nonspecific assignments, have you considered your own interests, any knowledge about the topic you may have, or your own expectations?

❑ Have you determined scope and tone?

THE ART OF TAKING GOOD NOTES

> *When found, make a note of.*
> —CHARLES DICKENS

Taking good notes on theatre is an art unto itself. Read (or watch) with a pencil in hand and use it. Marginalia (those little notes made in the margins of books by engaged readers) are a great resource when you are thinking through your ideas. If you are using a text that you can't write in, such as a library book or the Internet, keep a piece of paper handy and write down your reactions. If you are watching a performance and feel especially inspired by something, note your impressions on anything handy (including a program!). Taking notes when *reading* a play is clearly much easier than taking notes while (or just after) *watching* a performance. Live theatre takes place in real time; it proceeds apace and does not wait for you to jot down your observations. Plays on the page "stay still," ready to begin again when you resume reading and available to refer to again and again. Whether you are reading a play or watching it, notice your reactions: Do you find a particular character funny, boring, annoying? Is there a moment in the production or text that takes your breath away, that has you on the edge of your seat, or that is monotonous, dull, or offensive? Does something bewilder you? Make a note of it.

When taking notes while *watching* a play

- focus on your own reactions and key effects, scenes, or characters;
- be selective; do not try to take notes on everything; and
- take notes as soon as possible, during intermission or right after the performance, before your impressions get cold (scribbling in the dark is acceptable if you do not do too much of it; do not distract yourself from the rhythm of the production or from your experience as a spectator).

When taking notes while *reading* a play

- underline or highlight passages that puzzle or especially interest you (or note page and line numbers on separate sheet);
- note staging or casting possibilities that you think might work well;
- mark any vocabulary you are not sure of and look it up;
- if available (in anthology, play text, or playbill), use glossaries and other annotations; and
- write down your impressions a bit more fully in whatever form you like (no one else will see them) after your first reading.

For example, a student *reading Romeo and Juliet* might write these notes in the margins of the text:

- My favorite character, Friar—tragic or comic? Should be chubby/bald
- Tybalt more interesting than Romeo; cast a taller actor for Romeo?
- Especially good themes/contrasts: nurse/mother, dark/light, night/day, sun/moon
- Death scene so sad—daggers/poison should be shiny, noticeable

Watching a play demands a faster method of note taking since the performance unfolds in real time, with no self-imposed "breaks" to allow you to think through your ideas while you are watching. For example, a student *watching* a performance of *Romeo and Juliet* might take a moment during intermission to write the following notes:

- Red everywhere—why?
- Fight scene—Romeo smiling—reason?
- Costumes look more Roman than Renaissance
- Flute music—melancholy

Being overly analytical while watching a play interferes with your own emotional response to the piece, which can, after all, be the most important piece of "research" you can do for your paper. This means being somewhat selective in choosing what to note down at the performance. Especially if you are new to the experience of watching live theatre, you may choose *not* to take notes during the performance. This is perfectly fine, *as long as you write something about the experience as soon as possible afterward* (or during intermission), when your memories and perceptions about what you have just seen are clearest.

Noting Dialogue

If there is a key phrase or sentence that you wish to note, copy it down as exactly as you can. When reading a play, this is of course quite easy to do. However, if you are watching a play in performance and the phrase goes by too quickly to be recalled, write down its essence. For example, in Oscar Wilde's *The Importance of Being*

Earnest, Cecily says, "You must not laugh at me, darling, but it had always been a girlish dream of mine to love someone whose name was Ernest." Your notes on this line of dialogue might look like this:

> Cecily—act 3—"always wanted love man named Ernest"—tie-in with play's title

If the play is in print, always go back to the play and make sure your memory of the line is correct.

A System of Notation for the Proscenium Stage

One of the most useful things your notes can do for you when you are watching a live performance is to bring back specific stage pictures as clearly as possible; they can accurately describe what you see, hear, or feel when watching a play. It can be very important to note the physical (and aural) arrangement of the stage picture because these "pictures" often contain crucial information about a character, theme, or overall interpretation. If you write about a particular theme or motif, for example, describe how that theme or motif is actualized on the stage—what it *looks* like. Patterns, echoes, design elements, and other factors in the staging hold important clues to many artistic aspects of the production, such as the director's interpretation, the actor's approach to character, and perhaps even the playwright's overall "message."

But how does one note the exact location and arrangement of the stage picture without taking too much time out from other observations? By learning a kind of "theatrical shorthand," you can do just that. Maximize your notes' potential to quickly describe a stage picture by familiarizing yourself with the system below.

The following terms refer to positions on a traditional *proscenium* stage, which has breadth (from side to side) and depth (from front to back). In the glossary, there are descriptions of different kinds of stages used in contemporary theatre. Here it will suffice to say that the proscenium stage is still the kind that is most commonly in use, both in professional and in amateur theatre. It is a framed, raised rectangular platform that is three-dimensional, with offstage "wing" space that is invisible to the audience. This area is used to hide stage sets, machinery, properties, and actors waiting for their entrances. Once you have learned the terminology to describe stage positions for the proscenium stage, you may transfer that understanding to other kinds of stages.

For many hundreds of years, proscenium stages were *raked*, that is, built on an incline so that the back of the stage was steeper and taller than the front. On a raked stage, actors literally had to climb *up* the stage as they walked toward the back wall (hence the term designating that area, "upstage") and down again as they walked toward the audience (hence "downstage"). (See Figure 2a.)

To describe actors' positions onstage, use these abbreviations:

US (upstage): Actor is near the "back wall" of the stage.

DS (downstage): Actor is near the audience.

CS (center stage): Actor occupies the center of the stage.

SR (stage right): Area *to the actor's right* as he or she stands facing the audience (which, from the audience's perspective, is on the left).

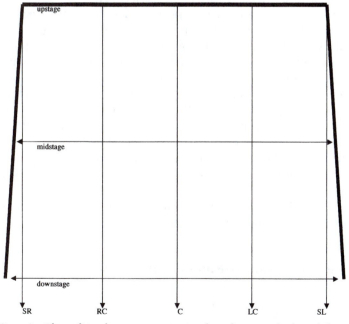

Figure 2a. The traditional proscenium stage is a three-dimensional cube with five main horizontal and three main vertical positions.

SL (stage left): Area *to the actor's* left (on the audience's right).

MS (midstage): Middle plane of the stage.

Combinations of the above can help you precisely "locate" actors or set pieces. For example, UR (upstage right) tells you that the actor is occupying the area by the "back wall" (upstage) and to the actor's right (our left). DSL (downstage left) tells you that the actor occupies an area of the stage closest to the audience and to the actor's left (our right). Furthermore, it is possible to categorize the actor's body position with respect to the audience. If the actor faces the audience, he or she is said to be "full front." If turned to the upstage wall, he or she is "full back." There are also quarter turns, half turns, and profile positions. See the diagram on the next page for more specifics.

Aside from the actual locations of actors' bodies and set pieces, there are other ways of describing stage compositions (i.e., "still pictures" that occur in the course of a scene). Several elements in stage design are used to create dramatic tension, but the three main elements are levels, planes, and diagonals. *Levels* refer to the head level of the actor. The lowest level is when the actor is lying on the stage, the midlevel is when he or she is sitting, and the highest is when he or she is standing. *Planes* refer to the depth of space on the stage, that is, from front to back. Generally speaking, an interesting composition is one that takes advantage of a variety of planes and levels in the telling of the story. *Diagonals* are a principal of stage arrangement that creates dramatic tension. For instance, three people talking to each other naturally form a triangle since that is the most logical arrangement if three people want to make continuous eye contact. Triangles and diagonals are also the best way for audiences to see arrangements with multiple characters, too.

The diagram on next page illustrates more ways to identify actors' body positions on the stage (see Figure 2b):

Sample Demonstration of the System of Notation at Work

The following example illustrates how notes can provide an accurate *description of the stage picture* and how these notes can then be used to develop a topic (or provide support for an argument) in

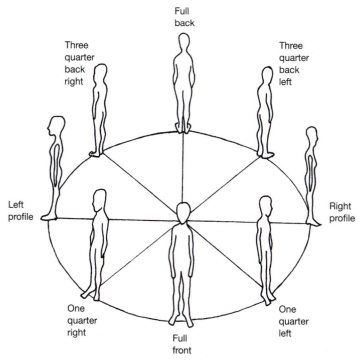

Figure 2b. The writer can convey important information about the play by accurately describing the positions of the actors' bodies onstage.

an essay. A student attending a production of Shakespeare's *Othello* used the notation system to help him remember the way in which the climactic scene in the play was staged when Othello murders his innocent wife Desdemona in a jealous rage. The notes looked like this:

Desdemona asleep on angled bed, DL corner

Othello watches, UR of bed

Chinese screen DCL

"Moonlight" from UR

Noises from soldiers, off

Soldiers enter through audience

Sample Demonstration of Using Notes in an Essay

The student wrote an essay titled "Public and Private Space in a Contemporary *Othello*" for his upper-level theatre course. In it, he used the famous moment described on previous page to support the essay's argument. The student "showed" how Othello murdered Desdemona behind a screen on the extreme left part of the stage and how the soldiers and authorities representing the social order entered through the audience. This moment was used as evidence of the student's contention that the production equated public space with disapproval and condemnation of Othello and Desdemona's mixed-race marriage and private space with the possibility of their love to thrive. Eventually, his notes about the way the stage picture was arranged in that particular moment became the heart of this student's paper.

Dan Huckleberry

Engaging title.

Public and Private Space in a Contemporary *Othello*

Opening paragraph is informative and engages reader with vivid description.

From the moment the curtain went up, it was clear that the Oblong Players' updated production of Shakespeare's *Othello* would highlight the racial aspect of Othello and Desdemona's marriage. Changing slides of famous photographs from the civil rights movement of the 1960s, including shots of Martin Luther King Jr. and Malcolm X, provided a backdrop for the first act. The play's settings, Venice and a seaport in Cyprus, were changed to resemble nameless but generic American port cities. The most striking set elements of the very first scene were two water fountains occupying the downstage corners, one marked "coloreds" and one marked "whites." Thus, the idea that there were different spaces for different races, but little to no room for a relationship of mixed races, was inscribed in the stage setting from the very beginning of the show. This paper will discuss how public space became connected with a racist disapproval of Othello and Desdemona's relationship in this production.

Introduces key terms of argument: race, space.

The story follows the evil doings of Iago, who plants false evidence to make Othello falsely suspect his new, virtuous wife Desdemona of adultery. He does this by manipulating an object from Desdemona's private space— her handkerchief—and placing it in the public space to condemn her, telling Othello she had given it to another man as a love token. This is one way in which the public space is used against her and against their relationship. Iago also literally crowds out the newly married couple into *Quickly* smaller and smaller spaces in which they can be content, *offers evi-* by interrupting them and preventing them from having any *dence from* privacy. There is literally no room for their mixed race *plot and* relationship in this production. They must meet at the sides *production.* of the stage for their all-too-brief, private encounters. Iago, on the other hand, has the full sweep of the stage and struts around like a general in charge.

The staging of the climax of the play, when Othello finally murders Desdemona, makes this point particularly clearly. A Chinese screen was placed downstage center left, literally squeezing their bedroom into a corner of the stage. A light from upstage right illuminated it, so the audience could see only the shadows of Desdemona lying *Uses more* in her bed and Othello hanging over her. While all was *detail to* quiet, he just watched her breathing, and started to cry. The *build* sounds of loud stamping from the public space outside *argument.* invaded and destroyed their small, private moment, and Othello quickly wrapped his hands around her throat and started to choke her, as if he had to do it before their privacy was invaded by the outside world for the last time. Soldiers then marched through the aisles from the "street," knocking down the screen to reveal the scene as she died.

Begins para- The director continually made use of these kinds of *graph with* invasions of their private space to demonstrate how Othello *broad state-* and Desdemona did not fit in with, indeed were victimized *ment, fol-* by, the public sphere surrounding them. She also impli- *lowed by* cated the audience in this public space since the agents of *supporting* a corrupt social authority, soldiers and senators, always *evidence.* entered through the audience space. The murder scene in *Concluding* particular illustrated how the public sphere invaded and *sentence* warped Othello and Desdemona's private space, where *restates thesis* their love might otherwise have had a chance to overcome *in more spe-* Iago's lies. *cific terms.*

This student discussed the stage arrangement and the actors' body positions at length to illustrate a thesis about the way public and private space function in the play. Theatre writing often incorporates this information about the stage picture, although the following example shows that professional theatre writers can often do so in a more succinct and powerful fashion. The following excerpt is from Kenneth Tynan's review of Laurence Olivier's 1964 performance in *Othello* at the National Theatre in London. It uses a brief description of the actors' body positions to make a point about Olivier's interpretation of the role. Note how the professional writer incorporates this important element of the stage picture, that is, the arrangement of the actors' bodies, to show why the writer finds Olivier's performance excellent. Here he discusses 3.4, commonly referred to as the "handkerchief scene":

> As Othello tells the story of this talismanic heirloom ("there's magic in the web of it"), we get a glimpse of the narrative spellbinder who conquered Desdemona with his tales. She sits at his feet to listen, drawn back once again into the exotic world of the Anthropophagi. These will be their last peaceful moments together. Her rueful comment on the missing handkerchief ("Then would to God that I had never seen't!") produces a sudden, terrific spasm of fury: "Ha! wherefore?"—the words detonate like thunder-claps. Before his exit, Othello repeats "The handkerchief!" three times. Olivier reaches a climax of point-blank intimidation in the first two, but for the third and last he finds a moving new inflexion, uttering the line like a desperate suppliant, whimpering for reassurance, his hands clasped before him in prayer.[1]

Asking Questions about Notes

Your notes on the text or performance will give you a good guide to your initial reactions to the play. After you've noted your first

---

[1] Kenneth Tynan, "Olivier's Othello," in *Olivier at Work*, ed. Richard Olivier and Joan Plowright (London: Nick Hern Books, 1989), 79.

impressions, asking another round of questions is critical to finding your topic. The two questions are the following:

- What function does this have in the play? That is, what does it *do*?
- Why is this important?

Your answers will lead you more deeply back into the text/ performance, forcing you to explain *why* something interests you, disturbs you, bores you, and so on. Once you can explain your reactions to yourself, you are well on the road to having a good, original topic that stems from your own interests. This section contains the questions you should ask of yourself and your notes as you find your way to a focused topic for your essay, followed by sample answers.

Question 1: What Function Does This Have in the Play? That Is, What Does It Do?

This question can apply to virtually any aspect of theatre: character, theme, idea, or design. It forces you to explain the presence of any element you have taken notes on that especially interests you and asks you to view it from the playwright's, director's, or audience's point of view.

Sample Answer What do my notes about the death scene in *Othello* show about the *function* of that scene—what that scene *does*? The scene between Othello and Desdemona shows that when the public invades their private life, Othello and Desdemona lose control of their world.

Question 2: Why Is This *Important*?

This question can quickly weed out observations that don't have the depth required for your thesis topic. Some notes are connected to the heart of the play, and some you can discard as useless on second glance.

Sample Answer The student's notes concerning Desdemona's death were *important because* they demonstrated how the interaction between public and private space in the play (civic space vs. bedroom) leads to some of the larger issues raised by the play, such as the relationship of the society to the individual and the fragile nature of love and its capacity to be destroyed by evil.

✔ *A Checklist for Taking Good Notes*

❑   Have you focused on your own reactions (e.g., things that annoy, astonish, delight, bore, or puzzle you) and on key moments and effects?

❑   Have you taken notes (or fleshed out briefly scribbled ones) as soon as possible after watching a live production?

❑   Have you used glossaries and dictionaries to look up words or phrases you are unfamiliar with?

❑   Have you noted lines of dialogue, body positions, and stage compositions for important moments in a live production?

❑   Have you asked yourself questions (What function does it have? What does it do? Why is it important?) about particular themes, images, relationships, or actions that you have noted about a production or play text?

WRITING THE ESSAY

> *He who has hit upon a subject suited to his powers will never fail to find eloquent words and lucid arrangement.*
> —HORACE, *DE ARTE POETICA*

Finding a Thesis Statement

After interpreting the assignment carefully, determining its appropriate scope and tone, taking good notes, and asking questions of them (What does this do? Why is it important?), you are ready to write, ready to shape your material into a coherent and convincing *argument*. An essay is an argument about your point of view on a particular topic. A crucial step in writing an effective essay is to choose a good topic and express it succinctly in a well-developed *thesis statement*. This section deals with ways to develop your ideas so that you can make them work for you. It also contains concrete examples of this process at work.

The *thesis statement* contains the main idea of your essay. It normally appears somewhere in the first page (often as the last sentence of the first paragraph) and has two primary requirements: it needs to interest the reader, and it needs to be small or "focused" enough to be thoroughly argued or "proven" in the number of pages assigned. Some examples of thesis statements for an introductory theatre class follow:

- An examination of the last scene in *Hamlet* in which Ophelia and Hamlet are alone together (act III, scene I) shows that Hamlet spurns Ophelia only to protect her from his own increasing instability.
- Money is a negative influence in *Romeo and Juliet*: poor characters like the Friar and Juliet's nurse are shown to be more sensible and sensitive than their blindly feuding, wealthier upper-class patrons and employers.
- In *The Glass Menagerie*, Laura's delicate glass animals represent the fragility of her infatuation with the Gentleman Caller.
- The main female characters in *Death of a Salesman*, Linda and Willy's paramour (who is simply called "the Woman"), represent the two poles of morality in his life and in the play in general.

The essay expands, supports, and substantiates this main idea, and the conclusion restates it within the broader context of the information and evidence presented in the body paragraphs. Developing the thesis statement is thus the first concrete step in the writing phase, for without an organizing focus, any observations about theatre, no matter how insightful or groundbreaking, are murky and shapeless. Although the original thesis statement is likely to shift and evolve as you develop your essay, the first, main idea is an important starting point for the writing process. In the actual writing of the essay, the first step is thus to *generate a concrete idea about what you have seen or read*. Three main component steps can lead you toward that idea (and thence to a workable thesis). Those three steps are outlined here:

1. Document first impressions.
2. Reflect on your impressions by asking specific questions.
3. Create a workable thesis statement out of the answers to those questions.

Not all of our ideas about the text (or production) will be equally interesting or significant, and one of the first steps to finding the right ones is to jettison the ones that, for whatever reason, don't hold up. It may well be that, under the pressure of questioning our initial observations, they crumble. If this happens or if you feel you have truly come up with absolutely *nothing* of interest, it's time to reread the play or see it again. A second reading (or viewing) often brings up things that you do not notice on the first.

Sometimes it's not possible to revisit the subject material; for example, you may be writing a review of a show that closed the night after you saw it. If it's impossible to watch a production a second time, then read the play or, if possible, perhaps read some critical material *about* the play, instead. Don't worry—it's not always possible to generate a workable thesis statement after a first reading or a first trip to the theatre. Simply go back and keep your mind open to every possibility, ready to take new notes.

Sample Demonstration of Finding a Thesis Statement Let's say that you are assigned a nonspecific essay for a wide-ranging Theatre Arts class and you choose to work with a play you particularly enjoyed reading for the class, Ibsen's *A Doll's House.* You attempt to generate a good topic by performing the prewriting steps described above. After asking yourself what your own interests were, you have jotted down that you are interested in family relationships. Since this play is about a woman trapped in a loveless marriage, you feel this interest has something to do with the material under consideration.

After your first reading, you have many notes on what kind of *parents* Nora and Torvald seem to be. You are surprised and interested to find that the play deals broadly with the character of Nora, not just as wife but also as daughter, mother, and friend. You have especially marked the dialogue in the text that pertains to the theme of parenting, noting when the children are present and when they are sent away and briefly remarking on your reactions to this element in the margins (e.g., "Poor kids—kicked out again!" or "T. scolds N. like a child!"). These notations, as well as your interest in the subject, lead you to develop a preliminary idea about what you want to write about: "parenting in *A Doll's House.*"

Your observations allow you to see that, in scenes when Torvald and Nora are in the act of parenting, despite the fact that they may look and sound like the perfect parents, they end up either sending the children away or in other ways failing them. This general observation already provides you with an "angle" or a "way into" this subject. You then decide that perhaps Ibsen shows Torvald and Nora in an *ironic* light as parents. You resolve to use this concept as your organizing thesis statement. You remain open to new revelations as you work through the process of writing, but this thesis statement, "Parental roles are ironic in *A Doll's House*," supplies you with a good solid starting point. The important thing is that you write down these statements as they occur to you, and as your thinking about the subject deepens and grows, so will your statements.

Your thinking will become more refined and specific as you continue to ask questions and revisit your notes and subject matter (the play or production under consideration). Documenting your first impressions and asking good questions will guide you toward an informed *opinion* of the work, one that both grows out of and leads into your *topic*. Writing the essay will be a process of testing that opinion against other possible interpretations by culling details from the text/performance (or other sources) that substantiate or support your opinion. Always acknowledge the possibility of an opposing point of view on the same material (perhaps your first impressions might supply something like this) and demonstrate why you were not convinced by an alternative opinion. Hopefully, this material may ultimately be incorporated into the body of your essay, where it will also convince your reader of the superior weight of your argument. In this specific example, you went back to the text again to search for ways in which the parental figures in *A Doll's House* were *not* ironized but came away from that examination more convinced than ever of the worth of your working thesis statement, which at this point has evolved into the following:

> *Parental roles are ironically undercut to expose the hypocrisy of family structures in A Doll's House.*

Creating and Using an Outline

Once you have a thesis statement, even one that is still somewhat in the process of being refined, and have determined the *scope* of your argument (i.e., how deeply you will go into the details of your contention), you are ready to *outline* your paper. An outline provides a primary structure that will help organize your thoughts as you write.

Although the basic outline will almost inevitably change and evolve as you generate new ideas and insights in the process of writing, it gives you a solid foundation to rely on as you refine your argument. There are many different kinds of outlines that can be useful, depending on your own inclinations. The most formal and traditional outline includes full sentences to clarify the main ideas, followed by sentence fragments that serve as "subheadings" to support or extend those main contentions. This kind of outline proceeds in a linear fashion (see example A). Another kind of outline (less formal but equally useful to some writers), called a "bubble" outline, consists of a series of squares and/or circles, each containing an idea about the subject at hand and each linked to the main thesis in different ways (see example B). The following examples show the same paper outlined in these two different ways.

Example A: Linear Outline

I. Traditional notions of parenthood are ironically undercut throughout the play.
   a. Torvald/Nora appear to be good parents and partners at first
   b. Children sent away whenever important events occur—not really part of family

II. Nora and Torvald's relationship distorts what it means to be a parent.
   a. Torvald insists on being "head" of family, is patronizing toward Nora; but Nora is actually in control
   b. Torvald's treatment of Nora as "doll" parallels Nora's treatment of children as her "dolls"

III. Nora's departure from Torvald is also a departure from parenting, and her search for self becomes a search for new models of parenting.
   a. Nora moves from appearance to reality—from irony to truth (wants to change from false parent to true parent to her children through leaving)
   b. Conclusion: the theme of parenting reveals Torvald's and Nora's true characters, the hypocrisy of the social structures in which they live, and the main flaw of their relationship

Example B: Bubble Outline

The Bubble outline offers writers an alternative way to organize related ideas and insights.

Introductory Paragraph

Once you have your outline and have revised it in the light of second and third thoughts, you can turn your attention to the first paragraph of your essay. The introductory paragraph presents information about the work in question (author, title, and date of publication or performance) and puts forth the basic outlines of your argument concerning it. Without giving away everything about your argument, the

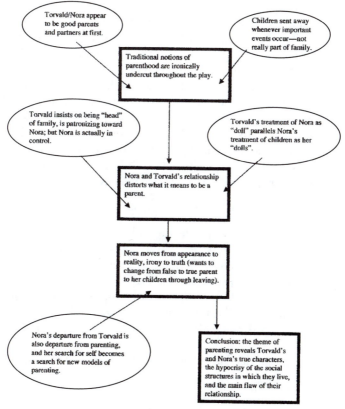

Figure 2c. Squares outlined in bold type contain the main ideas, and circles containing supporting evidence connect to the main ideas by arrows.

introductory paragraph should nonetheless provide a clear idea of where the argument is headed. It should also say something about the way in which you intend to go about proving that your contention is true, and it should catch the reader's interest. The following paragraph illuminates the function of the introduction (see Figure 2c).

Sample Student Introductory Paragraph

Henrik Ibsen's 1879 play *A Doll's House* was one of the most controversial productions in theatre history. Audiences of the time stormed out of theatres in protest, galvanized by the plight and actions of its main character, Nora Helmer. Although the play is now a familiar part of the canon of Western literature, Nora's decision to leave her husband and children still has a powerful emotional effect on readers and audiences. It is relatively clear why she leaves her flawed husband, Torvald, but her decision to leave her children is less obvious. Throughout the play, her identity as a mother is ironically undercut: treated like a senseless child by her husband, she is seen as progressively less and less able to care for her own children. This paper will examine the ironic way Ibsen portrays Nora and Torvald as parents and look especially closely at how their relationship with one another renders them unfit to be parents. By using evidence from the play and analyzing its emotional effect, I will argue that Ibsen uses the theme of parenting in *A Doll's House* as a vehicle for his powerful critique of flawed social and family values.

This student's introductory paragraph successfully

- introduces the subject matter (title, author, date),
- states the main topic (". . . Ibsen uses the theme of parenting in *A Doll's House* as a vehicle for his powerful critique of flawed social and family values")
- provides the reader with a sense of how the writer will go about proving the argument ("This paper will examine the ironic way Ibsen portrays Nora and Torvald as parents . . ."), and
- indicates what kind of evidence the writer will be using.

The student could improve the paragraph by

- providing a larger context for the argument (e.g., "Artistically and socially, Ibsen is arguably the most important playwright of the nineteenth century because his innovations made subsequent forms of drama and social change possible . . .") and

- giving the reader a sense of why the argument is important (e.g., "Ibsen's inquiry into the individual's relationship to social and family responsibilities remains a critical question for our own time . . .").

These changes not only would improve the student's introductory paragraph but would probably also help shape the entire paper into a more specific, grounded, and focused argument in general.

Body Paragraphs: Your Argument's Building Blocks

The midsection of your paper (i.e., everything between the introduction and the conclusion) should be tightly organized paragraphs that serve as the "building blocks" of your argument. They should each have topic sentences that are then developed in the body of the paragraph and be linked by transitions at the end of each paragraph and the beginning of the next. Each one should clearly build on the one before it: they make key connections that increase coherence and clarity through words and phrases such as "furthermore," "however," "finally," and "nevertheless." Transitions aid in clarification and help propel the argument forward toward its conclusion.

Presenting Evidence Each succeeding paragraph must support your argument with ample evidence to persuade your reader of the validity of your point. As Shakespeare's Fluellen pointed out in *Henry V*, "There is occasions and causes why and wherefore in all things." In other words, your assertions need to be backed up by lots of proof. Use convincing detail from the text, from your notes, from the stage, and elsewhere; in short, use every possible resource available to you and comb through it to find those items that are most germane to your argument. This evidence, combined with your own ideas on the subject, will be used in the body of the paper to flesh out and support your thesis statement. The most common kinds of evidence used in student papers, facts and quotations, are discussed next.

Facts "A little fact," Ralph Waldo Emerson observed, "is worth a whole limbo of dreams." Factual information (i.e., from outside sources) can and should be harnessed to support your essay. Depending on the type of essay you are writing, examples of good sources of factual support may include

- biographical details about the playwright's life,
- historical background and traditions associated with your topic,
- financial data about funding for a theatre's overall season (answering such questions as Was the production positioned as a subscription crowd-pleaser or as a bold, new initiative?), and
- information about the play's or production's principal contributors (playwright, director, actors, designers, and so on)

Any facts that pertain to your subject are potentially useful. Of course, you should only use factual information that is truly pertinent to your argument. Don't get carried away and try to include all the interesting facts you may come up with in your research; stay focused on those facts that relate precisely to your particular interpretation of or argument about your subject. Chapter 5 contains helpful information on methods and resources for gathering factual information about theatre.

Following is an example of how a fact supports an essay's argument:

> The movements of Noh performers are key to understanding story and character in this form of theater, especially for those who do not speak Japanese. The low center of gravity, sliding footsteps, foot stamping, and slightly bent waist may seem arbitrary, but all suggest a connection to the ground. In fact, Noh movements were originally drawn from agriculture, where growing rice seedlings required much difficult walking in mud. This tedious labor was alleviated by rhythmic movement and song, which evolved as a part of the Noh tradition.

Quotations Use quotations, either from the play's text or a secondary source, to illustrate main points you wish to emphasize. Careful reading goes a long way toward harvesting useful and appropriate quotations. As A. Bronson Alcott reminds us, "One must be a wise reader to quote wisely and well." For instance, section IIa of the outline for an essay on *A Doll's House* (provided above) claims that Torvald treats Nora with condescension ("Torvald insists on being 'head' of the family, is patronizing toward Nora"). When you get to this point in the actual writing of the body paragraphs, finding the right quotation will economically prove this point for you. To locate it, go back to the text itself or, if you have trouble finding it, turn back to your notes or marginalia, either from the production you saw or from the first or second reading of the text, and find the place where you first noticed this aspect of Torvald's character. In this example, the student marked the place where Torvald scolds Nora for eating candy. Here is how this student incorporated the quotation to prove the point:

> Especially in the beginning of the play, Torvald is openly patronizing toward Nora. This is never clearer than in Act I, sc. ii, when he scolds her like a child:
>
>> Torvald (*wagging his finger at her*): Hasn't Miss SweetTooth been breaking rules in town today?
>>
>> Nora: No; what makes you think that?
>>
>> Torvald: Hasn't she paid a visit to the confectioner's?
>>
>> Nora: No, I assure you, Torvald . . .
>>
>> Torvald: Not been nibbling sweets?
>>
>> Nora: No, certainly not.
>>
>> Torvald: Not even taken a bite at a macaroon or two?
>>
>> Nora: No, Torvald, I assure you really . . .

Notice how this student introduced this quotation into the paper in an interesting and logical way. Instead of blankly stating, "Torvald is patronizing. This is proved when he says . . . ," this student employed a more interesting and active "voice": "This is never clearer than in act I, scene ii, when he scolds her like a child."

Since quotations are such a powerful tool in building a convincing argument, it's a good idea to mark off the most potentially useful ones from the very start of your writing process. As you construct an outline, for example, make a note of possible placement for quotes that may be useful in proving the main points of each section. Writing "see page 10" alongside a section of your outline to guide yourself back to useful quotes later is a good way to cut down on time spent searching for supporting material after you've begun writing the essay itself.

When quoting a single sentence from a review or other textual material, use quotation marks and proper citation (see chapter 5 on documentation). For longer passages, indent and double space the excerpt. Quotations of dialogue from a play should not be enclosed in quotation marks, and the names of the speakers should precede the dialogue itself, as in the example from *A Doll's House* above.

CONCLUSION

The conclusion usually restates but also brings something new to the main idea first offered in the thesis statement of the introductory paragraph. Conclusions should always add to the thesis statement so that your paper not only proves your argument but also expands it slightly at the end. One of the following two examples is drawn from the student essay on *A Midsummer Night's Dream*; the other is a published piece by a professional theatre writer.

Sample Student Conclusion

In conclusion, Herbert Beerbohm Tree's 1900 production of *A Midsummer Night's Dream* made scenic design the star attraction. Audiences flocked to see it, and even though the scene changes could take as long as 45 minutes to accomplish, the sets were greeted with long ovations even before the dialogue could begin. From our contemporary perspective, the innovations in his set design have become clichéd: realism, down to real grass and actual woodland animals, no longer casts the same spell on an audience that is saturated with realistic images from film and television. Yet Tree's production reminds us that realism can be used to promote unreal, magical environments, and to describe intangible states of mind. In our own era of tired soap opera formulas, canned laughter and "reality TV," it is important to remember the excitement and wonder that Tree's designs inspired in the audience. I believe that, in the hands of a visionary and talented individual like Tree, realism could still galvanize contemporary audiences in the same way. We are still waiting for that individual to emerge on the contemporary art scene.

In this conclusion, the student reiterates his basic thesis statement ("Tree's 1900 production of *A Midsummer Night's Dream* made scenic design the star attraction") and then expands it to include a consideration of the value of Tree's design for contemporary audiences. The conclusion suggests a contemporary value for the salient characteristic of Tree's design (realism), "in the hands of a visionary and talented individual like Tree." By bringing the thesis topic (Tree's design) into a discussion of larger cultural issues (contemporary audiences), the student effectively advances his initial argument rather than simply restating his thesis statement.

Sample Professional Conclusion

Pathos truly is the mode for the pessimist. But tragedy requires a nicer balance between what is possible and what is impossible. And it is curious, although edifying, that the plays we revere, century after century, are the tragedies. In them, and in them alone, lies the belief—optimistic, if you will—in the perfectibility of man. It is time, I think, that we who are without kings, took up this bright thread of our history and followed it to the only place it can possibly lead in our time—the heart and spirit of the average man.[2]

Here Arthur Miller concludes his famous essay "Tragedy and the Common Man" by restating his thesis ("the plays we revere, century after century, are the tragedies"), then extending it to include a new concept: that tragedies can and even should be about the "average man." In our time, he says, a time "without kings," the only possible tragic hero is the average man. Thus, he succinctly sums up

---

[2]Arthur Miller, "Tragedy and the Common Man," in *Types of Drama: Plays and Essays*, ed. Sylvan Barnet et al. (Glenview, Ill.: Scott, Foresman, 1989), 746.

and extends his argument to include a larger consideration of the state of contemporary culture and the place of tragedy within it.

Drafts

Let your ideas flow as you write your first draft, and don't be too concerned at first with questions of style or structure. It would be a mistake, for example, to slavishly follow a preliminary outline. Of course, you will later revise your first draft, and will make sure that your essay is clearly organized. But while writing a draft, if an idea comes to you, by all means put it into words. Later you may move it or even delete it, but, again, while drafting an essay, don't hesitate to depart from a preliminary outline. The character of Belinsky, a literary critic, succinctly describes the hunger to write a first draft in Tom Stoppard's play *Voyage* (the second part of his trilogy *The Coast of Utopia*). Ideally we would all feel this same passion to put down first impressions at this early stage of the writing process:

> When a book seizes me it's not by the elbow but by the throat. I have to slap down my thoughts before I lose them, and change them sometimes while I'm having them—it all goes in, there's no time to have a style, it's a miracle if I have a main verb.[3]

When your first draft is finished, set it aside for a day or two if at all possible and then go back and read it over, pen in hand. Getting a bit of distance on your work lets you come back to it with an objectivity that will benefit you in the long run. At times, you must sacrifice bits of your favorite material as you sculpt your essay into a clean and powerful shape. Cutting out extraneous material always makes your argument stronger and your prose easier to read. Simplicity is a virtue in any kind of essay, and theatre essays are no different in this respect. Ideally you will budget yourself time to write a full second and even a third draft. Papers tend to get better the longer you work on them.

Whatever the approach, thinking about theatre that is performed, watched, or read and articulating those thoughts into a coherent written argument transfers the pleasure and the intellectual engagement of the theatrical experience from writer to reader.

[3]Tom Stoppard, *Voyage: The Coast of Utopia Part 1*. (London: Faber and Faber, 2002), 81.

As a multilayered, social, lived communal event, theatre invites you into dialogue with it. Use the tools outlined in this chapter, which call on your best powers of imagination and analysis, to articulate your unique perspective on this quintessentially human art form.

✔ *A Checklist for Writing the Essay: The Fundamentals*

❑ Does your essay have a thesis statement, a main argument?
❑ Have you tested your argument by looking for proof of its opposite?
❑ Have you used an outline to organize the structure of your argument?
❑ Does the introduction catch the reader's interest, state the main topic, and indicate how you will go about proving your contention?
❑ Have you selected well-chosen, compelling evidence?
❑ Have you allowed your ideas to evolve as you write?
❑ Have you written two or, preferably, three drafts?

3

THE REVIEW RESPONSE AND THE PRODUCTION RESPONSE

You see, if there's a point to writing, it really has to be the purity of creativity and getting in touch with the reality of those human beings, their flesh and their sweat, their nightmares and their hatreds. It's hard work to get in touch with all of that. But then once you're putting it together, the trickery of theatre is just delicious.
—MARIA IRENE FORNES, DIRECTOR AND PLAYWRIGHT

There are two main types of essays that deal most directly with the practical aspects of describing and evaluating theatre production: *the review response* and *the production response*. The *review response* is written from the perspective of someone watching a performance with the ultimate *goal of recommending it (or cautioning against it) to others*. The *production response* also takes the production's quality into account, with the *goal of demonstrating an understanding of the principles of stagecraft* (and evaluating them) as they are realized in the production under discussion. Note that the term "production response" is interchangeable with other terms in identifying this particular kind of writing about theatre; for example, it could be called a "production analysis" or a "reception analysis" by different instructors. Whatever the term, what is important to remember about this form of writing is that the production response has a different primary goal (primarily *to demonstrate your understanding*, secondarily to evaluate the production) than the review response (*to recommend/discourage attendance at a production*). However, they do have some characteristics in common; both the review response and the production response ask writers to articulate their opinions and then substantiate them with facts and examples, but to slightly different ends. In both instances, the writers move away from muddy or general thinking and toward the clear articulation of complex issues, demonstrating, using and expanding on their knowledge of theatrical practice.

Both kinds of essays are frequently assigned in applied or practical classes such as Acting, Directing, Design, Stagecraft, and Introduction to Theatre courses. They address what Maria Irene Fornes would call the "flesh and sweat" of production and are concerned with practical techniques and effects as well as with abstract aesthetic considerations. Since theatre is an amalgam of a variety of activities, learning and writing about it requires a variety of approaches to the subject, approaches that often go beyond traditional textual analysis and essay structures. This chapter builds on and expands the work of writing an essay (as discussed in chapter 2) by offering a series of examples and questions specifically designed for writers of these particular kinds of writing.

THE REVIEW RESPONSE

Reviews, because they regularly appear in most newspapers and magazines, are the most familiar kind of theatre writing. The reviewer's goal is to convey what the production looks and sounds like and to give an informed, substantiated opinion as to its merit. The review looks at theatre as an event, one that occurs in a real time and place. For the reviewer, theatre is an activity that is conditioned by many different things, such as the weather, the audience, the venue, and even the health of the cast (replacement actors can have a huge effect on a production). The review thus combines criticism with journalism, as it seeks to convey the individual reviewer's opinion of a play with a report of what exactly happened at one particular performance.

A *review response*

- conveys the essential characteristics of a production, including an outline of the story (if the play is not well known) and a sense of the overall quality of the production;

- gives an opinion; and
- backs up that opinion with evidence.

The best reviews convey the experience of being a spectator at a production in an entertaining or memorable way and indicate whether the experience was worthwhile.

Since the reviewer assumes that the reader has not seen the play, much of the piece is devoted to plot (unless the play is a familiar classic such as *Romeo and Juliet*) and overall theatrical effect. A good reviewer succinctly and economically describes the most important features of the production (plot, mood, and impact on the audience). Of course, it is possible to take this economy to an extreme: a London critic's review of a play called *A Good Time*, for example, consisted of the single word "No!" Try to articulate as precisely as possible *what* you liked or disliked about a specific element of the production and *why* you think you reacted this way, generating ideas about how the theatrical effect was achieved. As you read the example below, notice how professional theatre critic Clifford Ridley economically uses language to convey a sense of the plot, mood, and the effect of the production on the audience. His review is followed by "questions for critique" that will help you determine precisely why and how this review is effective. Read the questions and try to answer them for yourself before reading further. This review concerns a production of Tom Stoppard's play *The Invention of Love*, a complex play that describes the life of A. E. Housman, a man who was both a poet and a scholar (see Figure 3a). The play opens after Housman's death and takes his spirit on a journey of his past life.

Charon, the boatman on the river Styx, is missing his second passenger. A man named Housman has arrived on schedule, but the manifest for the trip to Hades appears to include two newly departed souls. "A poet and a scholar is what I was told," Charon says. "I think that must be me," responds Housman. "Both of them?" "I'm afraid so." The exchange occurs in the first minute of *The Invention of Love*, receiving its East Coast premiere at the Wilma Theater, and it's the seed of everything that follows. From one small but intriguing fact—A. E. Housman, author of the morosely romantic poetry cycle *A Shropshire Lad*, was also a world-renowned analyst of Latin texts—playwright Tom Stoppard weaves an intricate tapestry that is at once an antic socio-intellectual portrait of the Victorian age and a touching story of love and regret. Make no

Figure 3a. Learned (and winged) professors debate philosophy in The Wilma Theater's 2000 production of Stoppard's *The Invention Of Love*.

Photo credit: Permission courtesy of The Wilma Theater.
Photographer: Jim Roese.

mistake, however. The love story—really the anti-love story, for the love in question was unrequited and repressed—is primary. It's the ingredient that gives the play its soul, that sends you into the night quietly sorrowful over a life defined by a wound—and yet also with some admiration for that same life's crusty, uncompromising dedication to the pursuit of knowledge as an end in itself.[1]

Questions for Critique

1. Is the review clearly organized? Does it move logically from a thesis topic to a related conclusion?
2. Does it concisely describe the play's basic plot and/or theme?
3. Does it give a sense of what it was like to be in the audience?
4. Does it incorporate the writer's personal point of view on the material?

For this review, the argument is organized according to the spectator's chronological experience of the play: it starts with what

[1]Clifford Ridley. "Stoppard's Invention of Love at The Wilma," *Philadelphia Inquirer*, 18 February 2000, sec. W, p. 35.

the audience first sees onstage and continues from that point on. It introduces the main character and his initial situation and then moves on to comprehend the meaning of that character's life in the context of the total play. It does so economically and logically. Ridley conveys the essence of the play's plot (which revolves on "one small but intriguing fact" from A. E. Housman's life) and theme ("the love story ... is primary"). He succinctly describes the spectator's experience of watching this production (it "sends you into the night quietly sorrowful ... yet also with some admiration"), further catching the reader's attention by using interesting language ("newly departed souls," "seed of everything that follows") and by offering bits of dialogue for the reader to "hear." He clearly has a lively appreciation for this production (which he calls "a touching story of love and regret") and encourages readers to engage with the play by creating a vicarious sense of what it was like to be there watching it.

Now read a student's review for a class. After you have once again thought through your own responses to the above sample questions, read the answers provided in the ensuing paragraph.

Adam Graham

Review of Tom Stoppard's *The Invention of Love*

In general, the problem with Tom Stoppard's plays is that they are too complicated and hard to understand. That problem was in evidence last night, October 7, when I attended a production of his new play, *The Invention of Love*, at the Wilma Theater in Philadelphia. The play deals with the life of A. E. Housman, a poet who was famous during World War I (but not, I must admit, familiar to me). Although much of the theatricality of the production at The Wilma was interesting and entertaining, in general I left the theatre feeling frustrated and confused by what seemed to me an unnecessarily academic and confusing plot.

Housman is already dead when we enter the theatre, but that doesn't stop him from talking a lot. The theatricality of the opening moment, in which the lead actor is ferried on a boat hung from the ceiling, right over the audience's heads, saved it from being tedious, as he explained at length to the boatman Charon that he is both a poet and a scholar. During the rest of the play, he revisits his past and witnesses key moments in his unrequited and unrealized love affair with his best friend.

The lead actor, Martin Hoening, was excellent as Housman, and his younger self, played by Dean Whitman, was also very good. The actor playing the best friend, Alfred Petri, was not up to the standards set by the other two actors, and he has so many scenes that he generally lowered the quality of the acting. There were two long scenes that I found truly boring, one when the dead Housman tries to talk sense to his younger self, and one when he explains his passion for translating ancient poems into English. After a while, I got very tired of trying to understand the meaning behind the academic jargon I was hearing.

There were some moments of pure theatre that almost saved the evening for me. For example, at one point several famous professors from the past, colleagues of Housman, appeared onstage with enormous yellow balls, which they then tossed to each other as they said their lines. The scene changes were also good, with screens sliding silently and quickly across the stage area to reveal or conceal set elements.

In general, however, I must say that, if I had the choice, I would probably have chosen another production to attend. If you are very interested in Housman, or in the classics generally, then perhaps you would enjoy this production more than I did. Otherwise, I would probably not recommend it.

What can we say about this review: First, it is not particularly effectively organized because it begins by immediately attacking the playwright's work in general terms ("the problem with Tom Stoppard's plays …"). This sweeping negative comment detracts from the review's ultimate power to sway its readers because it is an unsupported generalization. Furthermore, although the conclusion is basically related to the introduction, the review's organization is somewhat haphazard; for example, he jumps from a consideration of the opening scene to a discussion of the various abilities of the actors (described in broad and unconvincing terms such as "good" and "bad"), then back to two scenes that he considers especially "boring." This jumping around and lack of detail detracts from the power of the conclusion to sway us to the writer's point of view. The review does give a vague description of the plot ("During the rest of the play, he revisits his past and witnesses key moments in his unrequited and unrealized love affair with his best friend"), but this description is neither concise nor particularly illuminating.

This writer gives a fair description of his own relatively negative experience in the theatre that night but indicates no sense of how other audience members may have reacted (Ridley, by contrast, indicates that the audience left with specific feelings of sorrow and admiration). Instead of using succinct and well-chosen examples of the production's strengths or weaknesses, the reviewer leaves us to trust implicitly in the writer's opinion, which is not substantiated. The writer does clearly indicate his point of view. However, again, it is offered without compelling evidence to support it (other than the reviewer's own boredom and frustration with the play's academic content), and therefore the writer's conclusions are finally unconvincing.

Notice the most important differences between these two reviews. The first review is superior in its use of interesting language to engage the reader and persuasive in its choice of examples that back up and validate the writer's perspective. The second review uses general language (this actor was good, that one was bad) without providing specific examples to support his assertions about the production. Whereas Ridley offers bits of dialogue, plot, and staging to briefly describe the play's effect on the audience, the student writer flatly asserts his own opinion of that effect. The first review provides us with information about the production that we can use to come to our own conclusions about whether to attend the play. The second gives us an insight into the writer's own biases, likes, and dislikes, but they are presented in such a way that it is hard to tell whether you might agree with him.

THE PRODUCTION RESPONSE

While the aims of the *review response* are to describe the production and to offer an opinion of it, answering the implicit question, "Should the reader go see it?" the *production response* has a somewhat broader goal.

A production response

- demonstrates an understanding of the principles of stagecraft and
- explicates specific successes and failures of a production.

Notice the difference in tone and intention between the student's review response above and the following excerpt from another student's production response, written about the same production.

Rachael Jones

A Production Response: Tom Stoppard's Spotty but Loveable
The Invention of Love

Tom Stoppard's play *The Invention of Love* received an excellent production at The Wilma Theater Thursday night. The strong cast and firm direction kept the wordy play understandable, and the set design was notable in that it single-handedly rendered the play's many complicated scenes clear and entertaining. The play revolves on the life of the 19th-century English poet and scholar A. E. Housman, who was already dead in the first scene, and who revisits scenes from his past as the play unfolds. The proscenium stage was raked to facilitate the audience's sight lines, and every bit of the stage space, as well as the entire auditorium, and even the ceiling, was used to convey the intersecting spaces of Mr. Housman's life. This excellent use of the stage and audience space to tell the story was typical of the imagination and creativity used in the telling of this particular story by the director, the designers, and the actors. In this way Housman's unrequited love for his male college friend is gradually and beautifully revealed within the broader context of the social and sexual restraints of his place and time, and the play is finally about the effect this tragic love had on his life and work (as both scholar and poet).

The special challenge this play poses is to depict two simultaneous time periods in distinction from one another onstage, while actors recite lines of poetry and ruminate on philosophy, creating a complex visual and aural stage picture that is at times confusing. The production's design addressed this difficulty by establishing the two "realities" in distinction from one another. First and foremost, the set design by Michael McCarty used different colors for the two periods, creating a kind of code that allowed the audience to keep track of these eras in Housman's life. Colors for the living were vivid and rich, while colors for the dead were dark and shadowy. For example, a bright yellow boat containing the young Housman and his friends contrasted sharply with the dark downstage corner from which the dead Housman observed them. Secondly, the young men's costumes were white and yellow, and the dead Housman's suit was gray. This code was also followed by the lighting design, which similarly helped establish a clear visual distinction that enabled the audience to read the scene correctly.

However, occasionally there were technical weaknesses, and the production overall was marred by a weakness in some of the acting, which disrupted the rhythm and tone of the play. While the lead actors had excellent English accents, for instance, the secondary characters were only able to accent a word or two within a sentence, creating the impression that members of the same family were from different nations. Also, the actress playing the only female character in the play (Elizabeth Hines) adapted a permanently puzzled expression, which made her seem the "village idiot" of the onstage world, for no apparent reason. However, the excellent direction created a variable rhythm in the staging that kept the audience engaged and distracted them from the unevenness of the performances, even during some of the longer monologues about literary history and the theory of poetry, when the attention of even the most ardent Stoppard fan might understandably be strained.

In conclusion, the strengths of this production outweighed its weaknesses. The Wilma Theatre welcomes adventurous and difficult plays such as this, and is willing to grapple with the complex and technically demanding staging this particular play requires. Although the entire cast was not uniformly up to the task, the design team, the lead actors and the director certainly were.

Like the review, the production response must be well organized, must touch on the plot and theme of the play, and must impart a point of view on the production. Additionally, the production response must *describe the practicalities and technicalities behind the production's strengths and weaknesses* in a highly specific way, demonstrating knowledge of theatrical principles and vocabulary.

Two questions help measure the level of achievement of any production response: Does it demonstrate an understanding of the principles of stagecraft, and does it explain specific successes and failures of the production? This response demonstrates a real grasp of the principles of stagecraft, in a number of different ways. For example, it describes the use of the stage space in the telling of specific aspects of the story ("every bit of the stage space, as well as the entire auditorium, and even the ceiling, was used to convey the intersecting spaces of Mr. Housman's life"). It also addresses the particular way color is used in the production's set, costumes, and lighting in order to "code" the dual time periods in the production ("The young men's costumes were white and yellow, and the 'dead' Housman's suit was gray"). This response also explains the successes and failures of the production by using particular examples of each and by linking those descriptions to the overall effect of the production. For example, the writer shows how an uneven, unexpected rhythm contributed to the total effect of the play on the audience ("the excellent direction created a variable rhythm in the staging that kept the audience engaged"). On the other hand, the writer points to certain acting challenges that marred certain performances ("the secondary characters were only able to accent a word or two within a sentence, creating the impression that members of the same family were from different nations"), which, on the contrary, "disrupted the rhythm and tone of the play." In short, this production response succeeds because it focuses on details that explain the way that particular theatrical effects were created in this production. Attention to the stagecraft behind the production takes precedence over personal taste in the production response.

The production response asks students to put their theatrical vocabulary and their understanding of stagecraft to good use to demonstrate a sophisticated understanding and criticism of the mechanics and artistry behind theatrical productions. It engages the total theatrical experience and gives a detailed explanation for why and how a performance looks, sounds, and affects the audience in certain ways. Although a production response *might* tempt a reader to go to or stay away from a production, that is a by-product of the writer's engagement with the performance rather than the main goal of the essay itself.

PREWRITING: QUESTIONS FOR REVIEWS AND PRODUCTION RESPONSES

Whether you are writing a review or a production response, asking questions will stimulate your thinking. Some of these questions you may only be able to answer *after* watching the entire performance, while others you should have in mind *while* you are watching.

Remember the importance of taking good notes (see chapter 2). It's always best to write extensive notes on the performance as soon after the performance as possible while the production is still warm in your mind. Waiting too long, when your impressions get cold, makes it difficult to retrieve the detail that will give your review or response the precision it needs. Remember that *likes* and *dislikes* are meaningless unless they are supported by specific detail that is convincingly argued. The statements "I like it" and "I don't like it" are never legitimate in reviews or production responses.

While the following questions will help you begin to formulate your opinion about the play as a whole, remember that you do not need to (indeed, should not) include *all* of your observations in your essay. You want to give the reader a sense of the most important production elements, but if you emphasize too many of them, you will run the risk of obscuring the main points of your essay. Choose your examples carefully, using only the ones that are most representative of the overall choices made in the production.

Acting and Casting

In the words of famous director Peter Brook, "The first step for anybody in a position of responsibility, like a director, is casting. Casting is where you begin." Casting occurs in several different ways and reflects the playwright's or the director's intentions or ideas about the material. Actors are often *typecast* (i.e., cast according to a physical type or behavior that the actor epitomizes in some way). For example, Nathan Lane, an accomplished comedian who speaks and moves rapidly and with great emotion, is frequently cast as a fast-talking funnyman, and audiences have come to expect that kind of performance from that particular actor. Of course, actors can also be *cast against type*, which means purposely casting *against* those kinds of audience expectations. An example of this would be casting a young, beautiful actress to play the old nursemaid Anfisa in Chekhov's *The Three Sisters*. This phenomenon is also called *cross-casting*. Other kinds of cross-casting include *cross-gender casting* (casting females in male roles and vice versa) and *cross-racial casting* (e.g., casting African American actors in Caucasian roles and vice versa).

Certain playwrights and directors have experimented with innovative cross-casting to create specific theatrical and/or political effects. For instance, in Caryl Churchill's *Cloud 9* (1979), an African slave is to be played by a white actor, a female character is to be played by a male, and a male character is to be played by a woman. In her preface to the play, Churchill explains some of her motivations for cross-casting these characters:

> There were no black members of the company and this led me to the idea of Joshua being so alienated from himself and so much aspiring to be what white men want him to be that he is played by a white. Similarly, Betty, who has no more respect for women than Joshua has for blacks, and who wants to be what men want her to be, is played by a man. For Edward to be played by a woman is within the English tradition of women playing boys (e.g. *Peter Pan*); for Cathy to be played by a man is a simple reversal of this. Of course, for both that reversal highlights how much they have to be taught to be society's idea of a little boy and girl.[2]

Questions to ask about acting and casting when writing a review or production response include the following:

- Does the style of a certain actor catch your eye (the way he or she moves, speaks, or gestures)? If so, why?
- What *specifically* do you like or dislike about their acting?
- Are the performers believable (do they seem committed to the reality of the given circumstances of the play)?
- If so, exactly what is it that convinces you of their sincerity?
- If not, do you think that their lack of authenticity is the result of a directorial choice, of an aspect of the play (e.g., surrealism may demand an unreal acting style), or of a lack of skill in the actor(s)?
- Do the actors' voices and bodies suit their characters, or are they purposely cast against type, and, if so, was that the right choice for this production?
- Are the actors' voices clear and audible? Can they be heard? (When asked what he first looks for in an actor, playwright Tom Stoppard replied, "audibility.")
- Are they talking *to* (not *at*) one another?

[2]Caryl Churchill. *Cloud 9*. New York: Routedge, 1999. Reprint. viii.

- Are they listening to each other or just waiting for their turn to say their line?
- Do they move well and convincingly, or do they seem unsure of themselves (and, if so, is this a choice for their character or a sign of being unprepared)?
- Is their interpretation of character in accordance with your own thinking about that character?
- Do they bring something new, different, or unexpected to the role?

Design

The design of the play includes all its physical and aural properties, including lighting and sound effects, makeup, costumes, scenery, set and properties (furniture and/or other structures or objects on the stage). A production's design can have great impact on the way the play affects the audience. Questions that will help you get to the heart of the effect and quality of a production's design include the following:

- Is there a design element that is especially notable (e.g., a recurring lighting scheme, a repeated color in the costumes or set, or a property that is repeatedly picked up and put down or in some other way shared by certain characters)?
- Does the set enhance the acting?
- Do the actors seem to "live in" the onstage environment, or are they separate from it?
- Do the costumes and makeup suit the world of the play? In other words, do they help describe or realize the characters and the onstage environment? Why or why not (be as specific as possible)?
- When do the lights change in color or intensity and why?
- How did the design (of settings, lights, sound/music, props, makeup, and costume) contribute to the overall effect of the production?
- Were there repeating motifs that gave the production cohesion (examples of a motif can be a color, sound, or even a shape that appears throughout the production)?

- Was the design purposely minimal?
- Was the setting neutral or abstract, or was there an attempt to reproduce realistic scenes?
- Was there a thematic and/or repeated use of any element, such as a particular color, light change, musical motif, or sound?
- Did any one design element create a specific atmosphere?

Directing

The director is responsible for the total coordination of movement, sound, visual image, and acting in the production. All these factors, therefore, bear the imprint of the director's vision of the play. The following questions are a way to decipher and evaluate the director's contribution to the overall effect of the performance:

- Is the director's approach appropriate to the material, or does the director's concept for the production interrupt or contradict the themes and/or ideas of the play in some way?
- Is the play performed in a traditional or in a nontraditional manner (e.g., a Shakespeare play placed in a gym or a Greek tragedy performed in the style of a circus)?
- If the play is new or unfamiliar, has the director told the story well?
- What is the style of the piece? Is it realistic (illusionistic) or antirealistic, and does it take place in a certain historical period?
- Does the director's interpretation arise organically from the material?
- Do you like/dislike the director's concept? Why or why not, specifically?
- Are the stage pictures (the way the actors are grouped onstage) pleasing, or are they (perhaps purposely) jarring?
- Do the actors seem well rehearsed? That is, do they seem comfortable in their movements and in their onstage environment?
- Are the actors (dancers, musicians, and scene shifters) well rehearsed?

- Is the blocking (the movement of the actors onstage) fluid and logical?
- What is the mood, atmosphere, or tone of the production overall, and did it suit the play?
- What specific rhythms or tempos did the director use to illustrate particular moments or moods onstage?

Venue and Audience

As actress and theorist Viola Spolin put it, "Time and thought are given to the place of the actor, set designer, director, technician, house manager, etc., but the large group without whom the efforts would be for nothing is rarely given conscious consideration." Just as the physical surroundings in which the performance takes place (the venue) are an important part of the theatrical experience, the audience for a performance can drastically affect the spectator's response to it. For example, during one performance of the thriller-mystery *Woman in Black* (a standard production in London's West End for over two decades), a group of American students who had never seen it before screamed in their seats as the scary effects and spooky plot unfolded. At the same production two nights later, a polite audience of older Londoners applauded lightly at the end of the show and only chuckled slightly at the same effects that had drawn such blood-curdling screams two nights earlier. Although the second viewing allowed the spectator to observe the production objectively, the first was much more emotionally engrossing and enjoyable.

When writing the review or production response, these questions will help evaluate the effect that the venue and audience had on your experience of the production:

- In what kind of space (venue) did the performance take place? Was it a traditional theatre, an art gallery, or a backyard?
- What kind of stage was used (see chapter 2 on types of stages)?
- Was the audience made to feel comfortable or uncomfortable in any way?
- What was the audience's overall response when you saw the production, and were you in general agreement with their response?

- Did the audience's response to the play affect your own response to it?
- Were the performers comfortable on the stage and in the venue, or did they have certain problems with it? (For example, some actors may have to struggle to be heard in certain outdoor venues or need to compete with sounds emanating from a nearby subway station.)
- Was the performance affected by the way in which the audience was seated? (For example, audiences seated in a theatre-in-the-round situation may occasionally lose sight of the performers.)

Idea

The *idea* behind a play is the essence of what it says as a work of art. The actions of the characters and the unfolding of the plot result in the main idea behind the play. Sometimes the play's title points toward the idea; sometimes there are philosophical statements made in the dialogue that connect with it (although most play-wrights attempt to cloak such statements in a more poetic or realis-tic mode since an obvious statement of the play's idea could easily ruin its emotional effect). To find the *idea* of the play, it is important to ask questions such as the following:

- Why does the main character take the specific climactic action he or she takes instead of another one?
- What is the result of that action?
- How does it make the other characters (and the audience) feel?
- Is the idea repeated in different scenes or in different ways?
- Is there any particular symbol (visual or aural) that points to or connects with the idea?
- Do you find the main idea meaningful, or is it on the con-trary trite, dull, or irritating to you?

Stating what the play is about in one sentence can also help you find the idea. For example, one could say that *Death of a Salesman* is about a depressed and aging man who withdraws into fantasy in the face of his failures. A statement such as this will lead you to a consideration of the effect of the play on the audience. Together these observations lead to the idea of the play.

WRITING THE REVIEW OR THE PRODUCTION RESPONSE

The process of writing the review or production response can be boiled down to these four general steps:

1. *Identify your reaction* After taking notes, asking questions, and coming to some conclusions about them, try to identify your overall reaction to the performance. How did you *feel* about the production? Did you enjoy it, were you bored, or did you feel uncomfortable? Even a preliminary statement, such as "Overall I liked it, but there were a few problems," can be helpful.

2. *Get specific: what did you like/dislike, and why did you like/dislike it?* Then refer to your notes and try to articulate exactly *what* you liked (or disliked) about the production; the point is to further explore your general initial impression. For example, let's say that in a production of *Death of a Salesman* you enjoyed the set because it perfectly captured the mood of Willy's world (you might even have an example of a specific moment where the world of the play was presented solely by the set, perhaps even before a single character came onstage). Furthermore, you liked the terrific lead actors because they were believable and sympathetic (your notes again may give you a particular moment of dialogue when this was particularly true). Let's also say that you didn't care for the lighting scheme, which alternated between extreme light and extreme dark, because you felt it distracted attention away from important scenes between actors and that the sound design puzzled you because there was a repeating sound of glass breaking that you felt was only vaguely related to the action onstage.

3. *Use notes to illustrate your points* Use your notes as you write about these impressions, without worrying about

unity or structure just yet. Concentrate on your reactions, using specific examples from your notes to illustrate your points. Separate these different ideas into distinct paragraphs. To follow this particular example, you might decide that your main idea will be *"the sound and lighting designs were the main flaws in an otherwise excellent production, and those specific elements interfered in specific ways with the audience's enjoyment of the show."* Try to gather enough convincing detail from your notes to prove your contention. If you can, follow that path. If you find that your examples are ultimately unconvincing, go back to your notes and choose another topic. Once you feel you have a fruitful topic, begin to make connections between your observations and structure your outline (see chapter 2).

4. *Find a main idea and refine it as you write the first and second draft* Remember that sometimes you must go through several ideas before hitting on the right one for your essay. If necessary, you may need to generate new ideas by rereading the play or by reading criticism of previous productions. If it is a professional production, you can almost always find out more information about the playwright, director, designers, and actors. Possible sources include interviews, reviews of other productions of the same play, or the playbill, which you should always retain for its useful information. If you find that a particular design element made (or ruined) the production, you might want to find out more about the history of the designer responsible, for example. Once you have a main idea and an outline, you can proceed to write a first draft of the production response or review. Refer to chapter 2 for concrete methods of developing a thesis topic and writing the first draft. Remember that in the *production response*, your emphasis will be on *demonstrating your grasp of the principles of stagecraft and the accurate usage of theatrical vocabulary* to describe (or critique) the production. In the *review response*, your focus will be on *conveying as accurately as possible the experience of being a spectator and on whether you recommend that experience to your reader.*

✔ A Checklist for Writing a Review Response and/or a Production Response

❑ Have you described the overall plot, theme, or idea?

❑ Have you described the key elements of the production?

❑ Did you incorporate your own point of view and how it felt to be in the audience?

❑ For a review, does it contain a final recommendation?

❑ For a production response, does it contain a demonstration of your understanding of the stagecraft at work in the production?

4

THE ANALYTICAL THEATRE ESSAY

VLADIMIR: *Sewer rat!*
ESTRAGON: *Curate!*
VLADIMIR: *Cretin!*
ESTRAGON (WITH FINALITY): *Crritic!*
VLADIMIR: *Oh! (He wilts, vanquished, and turns away.)*

—SAMUEL BECKETT[1]

Playwrights have always found ways to have their revenge on critics. In Aristophanes' *The Clouds*, a parody of criticism written in 423 B.C.E., the protagonist declares, "Now that my daily diet is Philosophy, Profundity, Subtlety, and Science, I propose to prove beyond the shadow of a doubt the philosophical propriety of beating my Father."[2] Samuel Beckett, in *Waiting for Godot*, demonstrates that calling someone a "critic" is the ultimate insult. In the academic world, the term is not necessarily negative. A critic is not simply a faultfinder; criticism points out strengths as well as weaknesses in a work. Despite these humorous jabs at criticism, it has always enlivened drama with fresh ideas and perspectives. Criticizing plays requires *analysis*, which is an examination of the relationship of the whole work to its composite parts. Analytical essays bring a particular, mediating perspective to the examination

---

[1]Samuel Beckett, *Waiting for Godot* (New York: Grove Press, 1954), 49.
[2]Aristophanes, *The Clouds*, in *Four Plays by Aristophanes*, trans. William Arrowsmith (New York: Penguin Books, 1984), 135.

of theatre, illuminating the work in question by pointing out qualities that might otherwise go unnoticed, and making connections between the play and the world surrounding it.

An insightful analytical essay does not simply point out flaws in the play or production under consideration; rather, it makes us see something in the play we probably would not have otherwise seen. The essayist assumes that the reader has some familiarity with the play under discussion, so (unlike the review) there is no need for a retelling of the plot. Instead, the writer is free to focus on a very specific issue within the play or production, on revealing details or ideas that may not be immediately obvious to the reader. They can be the most exciting kind of essays to write because they encourage the writer to work out unique or, at the very least, highly individualistic perspectives on the play yet also connect the writer to larger theatrical traditions, ideas, and histories.

TWO ANALYTICAL APPROACHES

We will focus on two basic approaches to writing an analytical essay about theatre:

1. Using the play's *form and content*, such as its structure (the way it is put together), shape, themes, or symbols, to analyze the way the play creates its theatrical effect and meaning
2. Using *theatre history* to explore the play's meaning in terms of its background and cultural underpinnings

Both approaches are concerned with how a play *means*, that is, how it conveys an idea to its audience, how it plays a part within a certain tradition, or how it mirrors the culture or time that created it. Each approach has *key topics for investigation*, which are questions and ideas that direct and focus the argument. The information these topics yield will help form the basis for your paper. This chapter also contains two sample student papers that both focus on Eugene O'Neill's *Long Day's Journey into Night* and excerpts from two professional critical essays, each using one of the two approaches described above. (Research sources for analytical essays using form and content and for those using theatre history are in chapter 5.)

USING FORM AND CONTENT

To get a good sense of what a play is *about* (what the playwright is trying to say), you must analyze it as a work of art. Plays are constructions, formal objects (texts) and events (performances) that are put together in a particular fashion, according to certain rules, traditions, or conventions. Some plays are constructed specifically to oppose and challenge those preexisting conventional or traditional methods of playwriting. In either case, a play's structure and content are essential to its overall theatrical effect and, as such, are fruitful subjects for an analytical essay. There are two subcategories within this critical approach, each of which provides insight into the way the play functions as a work of art.

Form

This category refers to the play's *shape* and *structure*, that is, to the way in which the parts of the play relate to one another to form a whole. (Important elements of a play's structure are in bold type.)

> *Key Topics for Investigation:* To get an overall sense of the **form** of the play, it is important to consider the following questions:

- Is the play broken down into **acts** and **scenes** (or not: some plays run without pause, creating dreamlike or other effects on the audience because of their uninterrupted flow)?
- In terms of this breakdown, at what point does the **tension** or **conflict** within the **plot** arise?
- When does the **tension** in the play relax?
- How many times does the tension fluctuate in this way?
- Does the fluctuation between the rise and release of tension or conflict form any kind of identifiable **rhythm**?
- Does the **pace** of the play (i.e., the **tempo** or **speed** with which the **plot** unfolds and with which the actors move and speak their lines) vary at any point?
- What is the **atmosphere** or **mood** of the play? Does it change? If so, where and why does it change?
- What is the **style** of the play? That is, what is the playwright's **manner of expression**? For example, is the dialogue dignified, slangy, choppy, simple, or complex? What is the effect of this style on the reader or audience?

- How do the **characters** interrelate to one another, to the plot, and to the **themes** of the play?
- Where in the breakdown does this interrelating occur, and what **effect** does it have on the spectator?

Content

This category refers specifically to the themes, images, symbols, events, and characters that appear (and do *not* appear) within the play and to the methods with which they are realized.

Key Topics for Investigation: To get an overall sense of the **content** of the play, it is important to consider the following questions:

- What if any **events** (or **characters**) in the story happen **offstage**, and why are they not staged? How do we know about them?
- What do the **characters** say about each other and about themselves?
- Do the characters' **words** match their **actions**, or is there a difference between what the characters say and what they do?
- What is the overall **shape** of the play? For example, is it short or long, does the climax happen early or late in the story, does it tell one single story, or are there many stories embedded in one? Is it balanced and symmetrical, or does it express only one point of view throughout?
- Are there recurring **patterns** in the language, staging, entrances and exits, gestures, settings, or other elements?
- Do the characters use **language** in varying ways?
- How is language used to differentiate characters?
- Is the play in **verse**, or does it use **everyday speech**?
- Is there a **subtext** (i.e., an **unspoken motivation**) behind a character's lines or actions?
- What is the shape of the speeches—are they long, short, or frequently interrupted by another character?
- Are there **pauses** or long **silences**?
- Is there any **pattern** or **rhythm** to these pauses or silences?

- Explore the text (including dialogue, stage directions, and setting) for repeated **imagery**, **symbols**, and **themes**. How does the language or the **setting** embody the **ideas** behind these images?
- Are there "unspoken moments" within the text (such as in **stage directions**, **gestures**, or **movements**) that crystallize those themes or symbols?
- What is the setting at the **beginning** and at the **end** of the play? Does it change? Why?

Sample Student Essay—Form and Content

Assigned to write an analytical essay in his Twentieth-Century American Theatre class, a student chose as his subject Eugene O'Neill's classic 1941 play *Long Day's Journey into Night* (see Figure 4a). He decided to analyze its *form and content* for his paper because he was interested in the way the themes of drug and alcohol addiction structured the way the events of the play unfolded. After reading the play, he took notes that he believed to be potentially useful:

> —Play's basic shape: structured into four acts, events build on each other
>
> —Plot unfolds two ways—staged events in time move forward, remembered events move backward to reveal details relevant to present
>
> —Addictions fuel memory/arguments about past, precede moments of highest tension
>
> —Events in play shaped by episodes of drug abuse
>
> —Play about the destruction of family/individuals, by ego and by addictions
>
> —Theme of addiction: cause or symptom?

In an English textbook, the student found definitions for a few terms he was unclear about (*subtext* and *symbol*). He made a sketch of the acts and scenes of the play and then marked down where the play's tension rose and fell and where drinking and morphine use occurred. This gave him a graph by which to read the pattern or

Figure 4a. Zoe Caldwell as Mary Tyrone and Michael Moriarty as Edmund Tyrone in the 1976 production of *Long Day's Journey into Night* at the Brooklyn Academy of Music.

Photo from author's collection.

rhythm of the play's conflicts. He also reviewed a definition of tragedy. Then he read the play again, taking more notes and paying careful attention to the stage directions. He wrote two drafts and submitted the second one.

Michael Green

Title provoca-tive and informative.

Memory Drug: Addiction, Memory and Dramatic Structure
in Eugene O'Neill's *Long Day's Journey into Night*

In great works of art, repeated themes or images deepen our understanding of the artist's underlying idea. In Eugene O'Neill's 1941 play *Long Day's Journey into Night*, themes of memory and addiction work in two ways: they enhance the play's emotional effect, and they structure its action. Alternating between an uneasy present and memories of a traumatic past, the play's action unfolds in two directions at once: toward the future and toward the past, both of which seem equally doomed. Addiction (to alcohol and morphine) links past and present, and marks emotional transitions within groups of characters. This essay will trace and analyze how O'Neill uses these themes of memory and addiction to convey the emotional complexity of the relationships between all members of the Tyrone family, and to organize the events of the play.

The four-act play moves ahead in familiar fashion, with logically linked scenes progressing forward in the chronological course of one day. We learn about the Tyrone family as they bicker, commiserate, and commune with one another. As the day unfolds, remembered events from the past enhance our present understanding of relationships and conditions in the life of the family onstage.

Thus the events that unfold in the present are given context by events remembered in the past. These "pieces of the past" often appear in the shape of old, unresolved arguments that surface in the course of ordinary conversations, many centering on some perceived failure on the part of James Tyrone, the father. Some examples include memories of James's alleged cheapness in hiring a "quack" doctor for his ill son Edmund, his failed acting career, and his disastrous business deals. Above all, the present action of the play is haunted by the past miseries caused by Mary Tyrone's addiction to morphine, caused by another previous event, a traumatic pregnancy and birthing experience that tragically ended in the death of the baby. As a structuring agent, this alternation (between learning about the Tyrones in the present and learning about them in the past) provides a rhythm that moves the play from one episode to the next, revealing the disharmony within the family's relationships, and their personal histories, to the audience.

We first experience this characteristic alternation in the play's structure in the opening scene, which is at first

one of seeming domestic tranquility, but quickly turns
tense when Mary remembers a bad real estate deal her
husband brokered. Her recriminating tone changes their
affectionate exchange into a verbal sparring match:

> Tyrone: (*defensively*) I wouldn't say that, Mary. After
> all, he was the one who advised me to buy that
> place on Chestnut Street and I made a quick
> turnover on it for a fine profit.
>
> Mary: (*smiles now with teasing affection*) I know. The
> famous one stroke of good luck. I'm sure McGuire
> never dreamed . . . (*then she pats his hand*) Never
> mind, James. I know it's a waste of breath trying to
> convince you you're not a cunning real estate
> speculator.
>
> James: (*huffily*) I've no such idea. (15)[3]

This is the first of many transitions in which the
dialogue moves from civil chat to increasing argument,
resulting in the overall alternation that moves the action of the
play along. Yet each memory also enriches the audience's
understanding of the Tyrone family and its struggles on a
thematic level.

We are given insight into a character or relationship
when a disturbing memory arises, often when some kind
of addiction has been fed, which affects the structure of the
Description play by prompting the flux of tension. The rhythm is
and then essentially this: a scene of "friendly" mutual drinking (low
analysis of tension) precedes a scene of vicious arguing (high
what is tension), usually about some shared, sad memory that is in
described. some way unbearable to one or more of the characters.
This high state of tension leads to an explosive climax, then
to remorse and reconciliation, which is celebrated or
marked by more consumption of alcohol, and the cycle
starts all over again. Each act contains this rhythm. For
example, in act 2, scene 1, Jamie "catches" his brother

---

[3]All page references given parenthetically within the essay refer to Eugene O'Neill,
Long Day's Journey into Night (New Haven, Conn.: Yale University Press, 1955).

Edmund drinking whiskey and decides to join him. At first, the atmosphere is friendly and playful:

> Jamie: Sneaking one, eh? Cut out the bluff, Kid. You're a rottener actor than I am.
>
> Edmund (*grins*): Yes, I grabbed one while the going was good.
>
> Jamie (*puts a hand affectionately on his shoulder*): That's better. Why kid me? We're pals, aren't we? (53)

But as the brothers drink, the friendliness quickly turns edgy. One page later, they are discussing Edmund's worsening illness:

> Edmund (*disturbed*): I'm not. I know how rotten I feel, and the fever and chills I get at night are no joke. I think Doctor Hardy's last guess was right. It must be the damned malaria come back on me.
>
> Jamie: Maybe, but don't be too sure.
>
> Edmund: Why? What do you think it is?
>
> Jamie: Hell, how would I know? I'm no Doc.
>
> Edmund (abruptly): Where's Mama? (55)

More concrete details support expanded thesis.

This testy conversation then turns into a full-blown argument about their mother. Jamie suspects she has been upstairs using morphine, which Edmund denies, and Jamie blames his brother for leaving her alone. Memories of coping with her addiction in the past fuel their disagreement, and old resentments push the play onto its next crisis and episode. The alternation between present events and remembered ones, and between argument and alcohol, push the play forward in a relentless flux of tension.

First sentence of paragraph connected to last sentence in previous paragraph, then builds on it.

O'Neill controls this rhythm by using subtext early in the play to keep the audience guessing about the true nature of Mary's condition. In the first two acts, there are only veiled references to it, and the spectator doesn't catch on right away. Only by "reading between the lines" can we see that Jamie is constantly watching his mother for signs of the drug. We may see this subtext at work in his worried concern about her addiction in this exchange from act 1, scene 1:

> Mary: (*She stops abruptly, catching Jamie's eyes regarding her with an uneasy, probing look. Her smile vanishes and her manner becomes self-conscious.*) What are you staring at, Jamie? (*Her hands flutter to her hair.*) Is my hair coming down? It's hard for me to do it up properly now. My eyes are getting so bad and I never can find my glasses.

> Jamie: (*looks away guiltily*) Your hair's all right, Mama. I was only thinking how well you look. (20)

Well-chosen evidence from play supports expanded thesis concerning alternation in structure, morphine addiction as rhythmic element.

Although at first we don't understand why Jamie is so uneasy in the presence of his mother, the stage directions about the way this early scene is to be acted tell us that there is something to be worried about. Over the course of the four acts in the play, this subtext of anxiety gradually turns to outspoken despair. This is yet another way that the theme of addiction helps structure the play. For example, in act 1, Jamie and his father try to reassure one another with veiled references to Mary's condition:

> Jamie: (*hesitantly*) Outside of nerves, she seems perfectly all right this morning.

> Tyrone: (*with hearty confidence now*) Never better. She's full of fun and mischief. (37)

By the end of act 3, however, this mutual self-deception has completely dissolved, and the problem has come out in the open, as we see when Edmund confronts his mother bitterly: "It's pretty hard to take at times, having a dope fiend for a mother!" (120). The pain of this direct encounter only causes Mary to go back upstairs to take more morphine. The whole family is caught in an alternating cycle of addiction and argument, reflecting on a thematic level the alternating rhythm of the play's structure.

Because the play ends on this tragic note, it is clear that the family will never escape the rhythms of memory, argument and addiction that doom it. O'Neill's genius is evident in his profound insight into family dynamics, in his powerful but delicate rendering of human relationships, and in his control of his thematic material, which is so closely entwined with his structuring of the action. Not only do the themes of memory and addiction move the play forward, they also pull the audience into the emotional climate of the Tyrone family, to the depths of despair that plague them. It is never clear whether the addictions to alcohol and morphine are the original cause of their despair or only a symptom of it. What does emerge clearly, however, is that the rhythm of tension in the play is intricately related to memories and addictions. Like every great work of art, the play teaches us to see and hear in new ways; its themes and rhythms weave the play, the Tyrone family, and the audience together into a tight, tragic web.

Original thesis expanded once again to address emotional effect on audience.

This paper presents a clear analytical thesis about the way the play's content (themes) interacts with its form (structure): "themes of memory and addiction work in two ways: they enhance the play's emotional effect, and they help structure its action." It is well organized and illuminates the way these themes both structure the play and develop the relationships in the Tyrone family. It offers insight into the complexity of possible meanings this interaction might generate. In his discussion of the way O'Neill manipulates the themes of addiction and memory, the student also proposes why it is *important* by pointing out its *meaning* and expands on these ideas in his conclusion, demonstrating the broader implications of his argument instead of simply restating his thesis: "Like every great work of art, the play teaches us to see and hear in new ways." The critical approach (form and content) helped the student find a way into the play by following the recurrence of two particular themes (memory and addiction). This led to a new understanding of the way the plot unfolds and of the way the play achieves its emotional effect. His analysis speaks directly to *how* it *means* something to its audience or reader. For this reason, the paper ultimately achieves the goal of the analytical essay.

Sample Professional Essay—Form and Content

Like the student writer who wrote the previous analytic essay, the professional theatre scholar S. F. Johnson examines the form and content of a play, in this case Shakespeare's *Julius Caesar*. Notice that by framing his critique this way, he too is able to discuss the potential meaning of the play.

> *Julius Caesar* has been widely acclaimed for its essential truth to the spirit of ancient Rome. . . . Even the style of the play seems to reflect a similar intention. It is unusually straightforward, having neither the lyric floridity of the earlier tragedies nor the condensed metaphoric texture of the later plays. The animal and hunting imagery is as forthright in its application as the frequent use of monosyllabic lines is forceful in its simplicity. Shakespeare subordinated poetry to rhetoric to gain his Roman effects. Rhetoric, the art of persuasion, is structural as well as stylistic in this play: the tribunes persuade the people not to honor Caesar, Cassius persuades Brutus to lead the conspiracy, Brutus persuades himself of the justice of his cause, Portia persuades Brutus to reveal his secret to her, Calphurnia persuades Caesar not to go forth, Decius persuades him to go, Brutus persuades the people to support the Republicans. Antony persuades them to mutiny. This persuasion and counter-persuasion reaches its climax with the speeches in the Forum, the turning-point of the play, after which the spirit of Caesar dominates and the Republic, along with the Republicans, is destroyed. . . . As the play presents it, however, the triumph of Caesarism is a matter only of history making tragedy ironic. There is no restoration of a positive moral order to relieve the sense of tragic waste.[4]

Note that Johnson does not outline the plot of *Julius Caesar* or "review" it in any way. He assumes that the reader has some familiarity with the play or else soon will have. He concentrates on describing its formal qualities to get at something subtle but complex about the

[4]S. F. Johnson, "Introduction to *Julius Caesar*," in *William Shakespeare: The Complete Works*, ed. Alfred Harbage (Baltimore: Penguin Books, 1969), 897.

way the play affects the audience and about the way it conveys its meaning. Specifically, he argues that Shakespeare employs an unusual form, a "Roman style," that stresses simplicity and rhetoric instead of beautiful imagery to convey the play's action and character ("Rhetoric, the art of persuasion, is structural as well as stylistic in this play"). Out of this analysis of the play's form (the way it is put together), he develops an argument about how the shape and content of the play create meaning: the audience is ultimately left with a dark vision in which there is no "positive moral order," only a sense of "tragic waste."

USING THEATRE HISTORY

Investigating the history of a play or playwright gives you insight into the ideas, conditions, and material pressures that helped shape the play when it was written and first performed. Situating the dramatist or play within a specific historical and cultural environment allows you to formulate a meaningful argument because understanding the influences affecting the play and its creator helps you determine what and how the play means to both original and contemporary audiences and readers. There are three main categories of theatre history, each of which provides specific information that creates a broader context for understanding and writing about the play and/or playwright.

The Biographical Context

This category includes all available information about the playwright's life.

Key Topics for Investigation:

- At what point in the **playwright's career** did he or she write the play under discussion, and how does it compare with the rest of the writer's work?
- What were the relevant **circumstances affecting the playwright's life** at the time he or she wrote this play?
- How does this play **compare with other plays by this playwright** in terms of its subject, structure, or theme?

- Was the play a **commercial or critical success or failure**, and how did that affect the playwright's subsequent work?
- Was the playwright using the play to work out or **experiment with any specific idea or artistic concept**?

The Social Context

This category refers to the society in which the playwright lived and worked, to the daily life of the people of the time, and to the social systems (such as government and the law) and institutions (such as education and religion) that regulated them.

Key Topics for Investigation:

- What was happening in the playwright's country (or, more locally, city or town) at the time the play was written?
- Were there **wars**, **pestilence**, **natural disasters**, or (conversely) times of great **prosperity** in recent memory?
- Was **religion** a powerful force in society, and, if so, what was the playwright's relationship to it?
- What was the **condition of the audience**? Were they generally healthy, oppressed, prosperous, or poor? What was the level of their **education**, and how many different kinds of people saw the play?
- What was the **political framework** under which the playwright lived and worked?
- Was the writer reacting against any particular **social condition**?
- What was the **ethical climate** of that particular time and place?

The Artistic Context

This category examines the artistic traditions, movements, and innovations informing the playwright's time and locale.

Key Topics for Investigation:

- What were the **major artistic movements** in the theatre at the time the playwright was writing?

- Was the play a departure from **existing norms** in playwriting, or did it conform to dramatic traditions that held sway at that time?
- What were the movements informing the **other arts**, including painting, poetry, literature, and music?
- Was the playwright an **innovator**, and, if so, what specific innovations are contained in the play under discussion?
- Did the play participate in (or, conversely, reject) any larger **artistic trends**?
- Did it **influence other writers** or artists?

Sample Student Essay—Theatre History

A student in an American Drama course was assigned to write a critical essay on Eugene O'Neill (see Figure 4b). Free to choose

Figure 4b. Eugene O'Neill, ca. 1930s.
Photo credit: Photofest, Inc.

any approach or topic for her essay, she decided to make *Long Day's Journey into Night* her subject, using *theatre history* as her approach because she was interested in how the play evolved within O'Neill's career and life. She read parts of a biography of O'Neill, consulted a theatre history textbook for more information surrounding the time and place in which he lived, and read about the playwright in a theatre encyclopedia. She then reread the text twice over, paying special attention to stage directions and the setting. The following are some of her notes on these sources:

—Son of well-known actor, addicted mother

—In other plays, experimented with different techniques; expressionism, masks, interior monologues to express inner thoughts of characters; used realism in Long Day's Journey

—Provincetown Players encouraged his writing beyond commercial producers

—Won Nobel Prize 1936

—This play more autobiographical than others—difficult for him to write—wrote only one more play before died

Here is the essay that the student later wrote.

Rebecca Howland

A Hard-Won Masterpiece: O'Neill's *Long Day's Journey into Night*

Eugene O'Neill wrote what is arguably his greatest play, *Long Day's Journey into Night*, in 1941 at the age of fifty. In it he examines a tragically dysfunctional family, modeled closely upon his own family. The play's overall theme, that people who love each other often also paradoxically have the power and the will to destroy each other, derives mainly from his observation of his parents' relationship. However, the play would never have been written at all if not for certain critical circumstances in his early artistic life. This paper will examine how the discipline and craftsmanship that defined O'Neill's adult life as a playwright merged with his deeply felt artistic convictions and his painful past to create a play that is considered by many a masterpiece of American drama.

Although he is the only American playwright ever to win a Nobel Prize for Literature (in 1936) and is now almost universally regarded as America's premier playwright, O'Neill's attempts at playwriting were not always successful. Theatre historian Oscar Brockett notes that, "O'Neill wrote about 25 full-length plays of uneven quality. Many were seriously flawed, and even the best often suggest that more was intended than was achieved" (Brockett, 551). Perhaps because of this tendency toward uneven writing, O'Neill took full advantage of every opportunity to persist in learning about his craft, and the high level of artistry evident in his best plays is a direct result of this kind of discipline and determination combined with his soaring imagination.

As a young man, after a debilitating illness, a deep depression and an unsatisfactory life as a seaman, O'Neill decided to turn to playwriting when his failed suicide attempt prompted him to reconsider what life had to offer. During the summer of 1916, in the small New England seaport town of Provincetown, he submitted a play to a small amateur theatre company called the Provincetown Players. They were a dedicated group of theatre artists who were intent on challenging current theatrical conventions and practices. They accepted and produced his one-act play *Bound East for Cardiff*, which was the beginning of a long and mutually beneficial relationship between the playwright and this company (Gelb, 98).

Without the support of this group, O'Neill would never have had the all-important opportunity to try and fail repeatedly, and to learn from those failures. The Provincetowners "wanted no publicity; they were experimenting for the sake of their own artistic growth and sought the sympathetic support of friends, not evaluation by Broadway standards" (Gelb, 318). He was fortunate in that these collaborators, especially Jig Cook and his wife, Susan Glaspell, were devoted to the idea that theatre should primarily be an art, and not a commercial enterprise. As O'Neill commented about Jig Cook, ". . . he was against everything that suggested the worn-out conventions and cheap artificialities of the commercial stage" (Gelb, 315). Their mutual admiration was a critical component in their ongoing professional relationship, and it allowed O'Neill to learn and grow under stable circumstances for a long period of time.

Although some of his early attempts were unenthusiastically received, Glaspell, Cook and other members of the Players continued to believe in him. Discussing his other two contributions to Provincetown's first season, a biographer notes, "Actually, O'Neill's only major contribution that first season, as he himself realized, had been *Bound East for Cardiff*. He preferred to forget *Fog* and *The Sniper*, and allowed *Before Breakfast* to be preserved only because he considered it an interesting experiment" (Gelb, 326).

As the company encouraged him to continue writing, he learned and improved with each play. They bought a small theatre on McDougal Street in Greenwich Village in New York City, retaining the name Provincetown Players, and brought O'Neill to New York as a resident playwright. They dedicated themselves to producing what they deemed important and innovative theatre, and O'Neill's plays became their most successful productions. They brought most of his earliest work into being between 1916 and 1922, and during that time O'Neill had the tremendous advantage of seeing his plays in production, which often showed him errors that were not initially evident on the page. Popular fare in commercial theatre at the time was mostly formulaic melodrama. Soon word got around among knowledgeable New York theatregoers interested in alternatives to Broadway that the amateur productions held in the small Greenwich Village theatre were interesting and different, if not always entirely successful. In many ways the Provincetown Players fostered his growth simply by providing him with a stage, a company and an audience, and allowing him to write flawed plays from which he could learn.

These fortuitous circumstances ultimately led to a mastery of his craft, which enabled him to articulate the tragic vision of *Long Day's Journey into Night*. O'Neill always made it clear that tragedy was the most sublime dramatic genre. In his words, "To me, the tragic alone has that significant beauty which is truth. It is the meaning of life—and the hope. The noblest is eternally the most tragic" (Gelb, 5). Called by *The Cambridge Guide to Theatre* "the most subjective of dramatists," O'Neill was following in the footsteps of his great mentor, August Strindberg, when he mined his own life, relationships and experiences for his greatest tragic play (Banham, 820). Using his own life as source material posed such a great challenge to him that he waited almost until it was too late to write it. In fact, he only wrote one more play before his death.

He had always known that he would write a play about his parents' tumultuous and tortuous relationship, and that writing it would be an ordeal. According to his friends, he put it off as long as he could. Only when he noticed that his stamina and energy were gradually declining with age could he bring himself to tackle the project he had so often imagined. Because he feared he might lose the strength to finish it, he worked at a fever pitch until it was done.

It is interesting to note that with this play he chose to return to realism because in the intervening years he had become a great theatrical innovator. For example, he used techniques of expressionism in *The Hairy Ape* and *The Great God Brown*, and used masks in *Days without End* and *Lazarus Laughed*. Critics have noted that when writing most closely about events from his own life, realism is the style preferred by O'Neill. This insistence on realism is a reflection of the writing process, which more or less demanded a psychological realism from the author even as he wrote it. His wife Carlotta makes this clear: "He explained to me that he *had* to write the play. . . . He had to write it because it was a thing that haunted him and he had to forgive his family and himself" (Gelb, 3). The reality of his own emotional intensity also gives us a clue about why he chose to write in the realistic mode. His wife remarked that while writing the play, "He would come out of his studio at the end of a day gaunt and sometimes weeping. His eyes would be all red, and he looked ten years older than when he went in in the morning" (Gelb, 6–7). The pathos the writer experienced while writing it translates to the reader or audience experiencing the play as a work of art.

Clearly, this play was his ultimate test as a writer, and perhaps as a person. I believe that he succeeded at this shockingly difficulty project because of the extensive preparation in the craft of playwriting that his long and early association with the Provincetown Players afforded him. Without that rigorous early training and the opportunity to learn from his own mistakes, O'Neill would never have grown enough as a playwright or developed the discipline to be capable of writing a play of this caliber. At first the audience attending *Long Day's*

Journey into Night wishes they could be a part of the charming Tyrone family, with its colorful stories, its banter, and its heartfelt relationships. By the end of the play, however, the spectator emerges from this play shaken and battered by the family's tragic turmoil, glad of the escape afforded by its end, but forever changed by having had contact with its characters. Because he combined native talent with the discipline he learned from the Provincetown Players, O'Neill was able to create a great American tragedy out of the materials of his own life, although at tremendous personal cost.

Works Cited

Banham, Martin, ed. *The Cambridge Guide to Theatre.* Cambridge: Cambridge University Press, 1995.

Brockett, Oscar, and Franklin Hildy. *History of the Theatre.* Boston: Allyn & Bacon, 1991.

Gelb, Arthur, and Barbara Gelb. *O'Neill.* New York: Harper and Brothers, 1962.

This student uses theatre history in two main ways. The biographical context allows her to explain how O'Neill obtained a mastery over his craft through his association with the Provincetown Players. The artistic context allows her to refine this discussion by exploring how the Provincetown Players specifically challenged the conventions and traditions of theatre that reigned during this time, so that she locates O'Neill in a particular artistic tradition and cultural context. She also engages both the biographical and the artistic context when she compares the style in which this play was written (realism) with other plays in O'Neill's oeuvre. Because she uses theatre history, the student presents a broad understanding of O'Neill's own personal, cultural, and historical moment and is able to discuss the innovations represented by the Provincetown Players in terms of their original audience. Although this paper does not make arguments about the way the play's dialogue, symbols, or other internal elements work to affect the audience, it does offer an interpretation of *how the play conveys meaning* in terms of the broader categories of history, culture, and the playwright's own oeuvre, and therefore it is a successful analytical essay.

Sample Professional Essay—Theatre History

In the following professional example, theatre critic John Russel Taylor examines the life of English playwright Noel Coward to better understand Coward's manipulation of a particular dramatic convention: the well-made play (the phrase "well-made play" refers to a particular kind of plot construction and theatrical effect; see the glossary for a more thorough definition).

If we examine the question in detail, it is obvious that what Coward was doing was reforming the well-made-play tradition to take out some of the literature and put back, not necessarily more real life, but certainly more theatrical life. And this depends first and foremost on a clear realization that plays are not primarily, perhaps not even significantly, for reading, but for speaking. . . . Coward's dialogue is not as it is because he has observed how people in real life speak and he has copied them, but because he has observed what works most effectively in the theatre and what does not . . .

To find out exactly how this reformation came about, and how Noel Coward by 1929 came to be recognized (by Maugham again) as the writer in English theatre exerting most "influence with young writers," so that "it is probably his inclination and practice that will be responsible for the manner in which plays will be written during the next twenty years," we must look in some more detail at his debut and early career. He was born in Teddington in 1899 and after various amateur experiences as a performer made his first professional appearance at the age of eleven in a children's play called *The Goldfish*. He began writing lyrics and composing songs in his teens, and had written two unpublished novels by the time he was nineteen. In 1918 he wrote his first play, *The Last Trick*, a four-act melodrama. It was turned down, amiably, by the impresario Gilbert Miller, who said that the dialogue was good but the construction lousy, and passed on the thought that "the construction of a play was as important as the foundations of a house, whereas dialogue, however good, could only at best be considered as interior decoration." The result of this was the immediate composition of three plays (Taylor, 129–32).

Work Cited

Taylor, John Russel. *The Rise and Fall of the Well-Made Play*. New York: Hill and Wang, 1967.

The author of this piece uses theatre history to explore his main thesis, which is to examine how and why Noel Coward "reformed" the well-made-play tradition. In considering how this playwright intersects with that tradition, he points out that when writing dialogue, Coward was more interested in achieving good theatrical effects than he was in recording "real" life. He looks to Coward's biography for information on how and why Coward made these innovations to the well-made-play structure. He discovers evidence, in the form of Coward's first rejection, of the discipline and determination that would propel Coward to the highest rank of playwrights in his day. For example, we learn that on receiving the opinion of Gilbert Miller that the construction of his play was "lousy," Coward taught himself about good construction by "immediately" composing three new plays. By discovering that he wrote plays virtually from childhood, we also learn that Coward was an extremely dedicated artist. In this successful analysis, Taylor succinctly demonstrates that a playwright's past—and his connection to a particular theatrical tradition (that of the well-made play)—holds important clues about the *meaning* of his or her writing style and general approach to theatre.

✔ *A Checklist for Writing Analytical Essays*

❏   For an essay using the form-and-content approach, have you analyzed the play's form or shape in terms of its composite parts?

❏   Have you analyzed how its formal qualities contribute to the play's overall meaning or idea?

❏   Have you examined the content (themes, characters, imagery, and so on) to discover how it conveys meaning to the reader or audience?

❏   Have you made connections between the play's form and content and any larger traditions, movements, or ideas?

❏   For an essay using the theatre history approach, have you examined the author's biography and playwriting career and/or the play's production history to analyze the play's meaning in terms of its author and original audience?

❑   Have you researched the social and cultural conditions under which the play was written?

❑   Have you examined any artistic traditions, movements, or trends that the play challenges or is a part of?

5

RESEARCH: METHODS AND MATERIALS

The way to do research is to attack the facts at the point of greatest astonishment.

—CELIA GREEN

Research strengthens all kinds of thinking and any kind of writing. An original idea or opinion about theatre is a powerful starting point, but research provides the rhetorical force that ultimately turns that opinion into persuasive argument. Learning more about your subject both expands your context and refines your thinking. To a certain extent, doing research is a normal extension of your natural curiosity about a subject. That's why taking the time to find the right topic is important (see chapter 2). When you find a subject that interests you, your curiosity can help lead you toward appropriate research materials. As Fefu in Maria Irene Fornes's play *Fefu and Her Friends* remarks, "I like exciting ideas. They give me energy."[1]

We can distinguish two kinds of essays: the thoughtful but simple commentary versus the paper that shows research: the well-documented, well-developed perspective that reflects an engagement with related ideas and histories. For example, two students wrote essays on a college production of Shakespeare's *A Midsummer Night's Dream* for an Introduction to Theatre class. One adequately described the staging and gave a basic overview of the plot. The other

---

[1]Fornes, Maria Irene. *Fefu and Her Friends* (New York: PAJ Publications, 1978), 9.

read about other productions of the play and discovered Peter
Brook's famous 1970 version, which featured a neutral set, circus elements, and uninhibited sexual farce, techniques that were radically
innovative for the time. She then read Brook's seminal 1968 book *The
Empty Space*. This student was then able to provide a critical and
theoretical context for the same production, basing an analysis of it
on Brook's theoretical conception of modern drama as an immediate,
harrowing, and collective experience. By incorporating pertinent
research into the essay, the second writer offered a more sophisticated, authoritative, and ultimately superior argument about how the
production achieved certain theatrical effects and how those effects
conveyed meaning to the audience.

PRIMARY AND SECONDARY SOURCES

Research materials are divided into primary and secondary categories. *Primary sources* are the actual documents or performances
being addressed; *secondary sources* are critical or historical documents (or other media) already written about those primary materials. Your engagement with the primary source is most important,
for your essay will ideally express your own thinking and ideas about
the topic rather than those of other writers. For example, Marsha
Norman's published play *'Night, Mother* is a primary source, as is
attendance at a performance of this play. Secondary sources would
include a review of the play in a newspaper or magazine, a scholarly
essay, or an excerpt from the playbill, all of which will give you more
insight into various aspects of the play and author. To study this play
in a general way, you would have to engage the primary materials;
that is, you would have to read the play carefully, probably more
than once, or watch the performance attentively. But if you wish to
write an essay about the play or playwright from a critical perspective, or if you wish to analyze a practical aspect of the production
(such as the acting or directing), you would want to explore more
sources that will broaden your understanding of the play or production, such as articles debating its merit as a piece of feminist theatre
or reviews of other productions with different interpretations.

Primary sources for theatre include all aspects of the production, from the sound, costume, set, lighting, and makeup designs to
the acting and directing of the show as well as firsthand accounts of

the practitioners and audiences who experienced it. These are considered primary sources because writers must consider them an integral part of the production apparatus. Because of the nature of performance and its limitations in space and real time, it is clearly not always possible to experience a live performance, especially if you are writing about past productions. Famed performances, such as the Moscow Art Theatre's productions of Chekhov's plays (as directed by Stanislavski), or productions featuring renowned actors in history, such as Ellen Terry, Sarah Bernhardt, or Edwin Forrest, not to mention productions from Shakespeare's era and before, are fascinating subjects to write about that can be re-created only in your imagination and through research, with the aid of firsthand accounts and reviews from the period.

Occasionally it is possible to watch a recording of a live performance on videotape or on a DVD. While watching a recording is a decidedly different experience from being a spectator at a live performance, it nonetheless allows you to witness the production as an event with spectators (a crucial ingredient in the life of a play). When writing about a performance you have viewed on a recording, it is important to acknowledge that fact in your essay, as it affects your response to the production in fundamental ways. The writer's relationship to this kind of resource becomes more complicated if the taping becomes itself interpretive, that is, if camera angles, lighting, or other artistic elements in the film footage actually comment on the production in some way. Again, under these circumstances, it is important to take the interpretation demonstrated by the director of the film or video into account as you write about the production.

WHERE TO START RESEARCH

- *Consult bibliographies and suggested reading lists.* Often the best place to begin research is in the bibliography or suggested reading list of the anthology, article, or other text your instructor uses in class. Sometimes those lists are found at the end of the entire text, sometimes they are placed at the end of each chapter or section. The authors who write and compile these books and anthologies are very well acquainted with the latest developments in scholarship and design their books precisely to be as useful to student research as possible. Suggested reading lists can save you time by making your research more efficient.

- *Use the Internet effectively.* Be cautious of general Web sites, such as Wikipedia and Google, that will yield too much potentially unreliable (and irrelevant) information about your topic. Instead, use your library system's online index and databases to find full-text or excerpted articles (excerpts are incomplete portions of the article or text) from scholarly journals and other useful publications. Use "findtext" and key word searches to help you find relevant material. (See the section "How to Use an Online Index" later in this chapter.) Web sites on or about theatre can offer many helpful links to various resources. However, remember that they are of varying quality and reliability and are in a near-constant state of flux. Here is a list of some useful theatre Web sites:

  http://www.americandrama.org
  http://www.curtainup.com
  http://www.drama.enserver.org
  http://www.muse.jhu.edu
  http://www.playbill.com
  http://www.backstage.com
  http://www.variety.com
  http://www.aislesay.com
  http://www.nytheatre-wire.com
  http://www.nytimes.com
  http://www.nytimages.com
  http://www.americantheaterweb.com

Other Web sites are available through various search engines, either with the key words "theatre research" or with the specific play, production, or playwright you are looking for.

- *Consult guides, encyclopedias, and theatre dictionaries.* The following is a sampling of books that provide good general overviews of theatre studies, history, and criticism. Although most will not contain specific arguments about particular productions or plays, all offer factual information about theatre that is extremely useful for beginning research for an essay about theatre.

Banham, Martin, ed. *The Cambridge Guide to Theatre*. Cambridge: Cambridge University Press, 1995.

Brandt, George W., ed. *Modern Theories of Drama: A Selection of Writings on Drama and Theatre 1850–1990*. Oxford: Oxford University Press, 1998.

Brockett, Oscar, and Franklin Hildy. *History of the Theatre*. Boston: Allyn & Bacon, 1991.

Brown, John Russell. *The Oxford Illustrated History of Theatre*. Oxford: Oxford University Press, 1997.

Carlson, Marvin. *Theories of the Theatre: A Historical and Critical Survey, from the Greeks to the Present*. Ithaca, N.Y.: Cornell University Press, 1993.

Cohen, Robert. *Theatre*. New York: McGraw-Hill, 2002.

Gerould, Daniel. *Theatre/Theory/Theatre: The Major Critical Texts from Aristotle and Zeami to Soyinka and Havel*. New York: Applause Books, 2003.

Klaus, Carl H., Miriam Gilbert, and Bradford S. Field. *Stages of Drama: Classical to Contemporary Theater*. New York: Bedford/St. Martin's Press, 2002.

Plotkins, Marilyn J. *The American Repertory Theatre Reference Book*. Westport, Conn.: Praeger, 2005.

Troubridge, Emma. *Scenic Art and Construction*. Wiltshire: Crowood Press, 2000.

Wickham, Glynne. *A History of the Theater*. London: Phaidon Press, 1994.

Zarilli, Phillip, Bruce McConachie, Gary Jay Williams and Carol Fisher Sorgenfrei. *Theatre Histories: An Introduction*. New York: Routledge, 2006.

In addition to books, articles, and Web sites, there are many other kinds of print resources for theatre research. Playbills from past or current productions (which can include accompanying director's or dramaturge's notes) may offer information on the professional experience of the personnel in a particular production and/or other salient information about their interpretation of the play. Mission statements from theatre schools, institutions, and companies may also contain useful information. Interviews with directors, actors, designers, playwrights, and other practitioners can often be found in the popular press, both in print and on the Internet. Journals, magazines, and newspapers contain a wealth of theatre reviews of productions past and present.

USING RESEARCH IN ESSAYS ABOUT THEATRE PRACTICE

Research contextualizes and invigorates the performance of a play, role, or scene. In the following example, Kenneth Tynan, literary manager/dramaturge of London's National Theatre during the 1960s, describes the way research and tradition came together to inform actor Laurence Olivier's interpretation of the part of Othello:

> The germ of this came from a famous essay by Dr. F. R. Leavis, which Dexter and I had already studied with Olivier. . . . There are moral flaws in every other Shakespearean hero, but Othello is traditionally held to be exempt. Olivier's reading made us realize that tradition might be wrong; that Othello was flawed indeed with the sin of pride. At the power of his voice, the windows shook and my scalp tingled. . . . I wondered at the risks he was taking. Mightn't the knockdown arrogance of this interpretation verge too closely for comfort on comedy? . . . Then he came to "Farewell the plumed troop," and again the hair rose on my neck. It was like the dying moan of a fighting bull.[2]

Tynan describes how researching F. R. Leavis's essay informed Olivier's choice to take a nontraditional approach to the role. Note that Tynan uses the same research to describe what was unique and original about Olivier's performance, which in turn affected the experience of being a spectator. This is a good example of how research supports both the act of performance and writing about that performance.

Students writing about various practical areas of stagecraft may use research to

- discover previous, alternative, or traditional ways of acting, directing, or designing a role or scene;
- resuscitate previous interpretations (e.g., when staging a historically accurate production of a classical play); and
- challenge established patterns of production (e.g., staging a classical play in a new way).

---

[2]Tynan, Kenneth. "Olivier's Othello," in *Olivier at Work*, ed. Lyn Haill (London: Nick Hern Books, 1989), 76.

USING RESEARCH IN ANALYTICAL ESSAYS

Research can strengthen your critical analysis. While your main focus should always be on your own interpretation and ideas, evaluating and incorporating what others have written about your topic can help you refine your argument or perspective. In the following professional example, the author quotes Henry James to clarify her own ideas about playwright Henrik Ibsen:

> Ibsen followed *The Lady from the Sea* with another portrait of a woman, probably his most famous, *Hedda Gabler* (1890). In spite of the fact that the subject matter is essentially undramatic, it has always been one of Ibsen's most popular works. Henry James described it as "the picture not of an action but of a condition"; yet there are few plays that have such power to grip and hold an audience.[3]

Here the author uses research (the quotation by Henry James) to indicate what is extraordinary and distinctive about *Hedda Gabler* and to distinguish her own perspective. This quotation balances and refines her argument about the play's power to grip an audience.

Students writing a critical, analytical essay about theatre may use research to do the following:

- Articulate and support their own subtle or complex points about a text, character, or playwright

    Example: "In his introduction to Miller's play, William Worthen compares *Death of a Salesman* to *Hamlet*. I would go beyond this general premise and argue that Willy Loman's self-destructive tendencies specifically echo Hamlet's suicidal indecision."

- Illustrate precedents they wish to adhere to or diverge from

    Example: "Tracing the construction of the plot of *Oedipus Rex* demonstrates why theatre historians and scholars frequently call it the most perfect Greek tragedy."

---

[3]La Gallienne, Eva. "Introduction," in *The Wild Duck and Other Plays by Henrik Ibsen* (New York: Modern Library, 1961), xxviii.

- Disprove the perspectives of other critics

  > Example: "Unlike John Barton, who claimed in his book
  > *Playing Shakespeare* that Shakespeare's plays can be
  > completely understood only in performance, I agree with
  > critics who believe that the plays are equally if not more
  > accessible when read as literature."

RESEARCH METHODS

Part of the trick to doing economical, efficient research is in knowing what *not* to research. Too much research can be as bad as not enough; it can confuse and disorient you, distracting you from your original viewpoint or idea. Here are some general principles for conducting your research in the most efficient possible manner:

- *Think it through before diving in.* Although you certainly won't have a fully formed thesis topic before you start your research, an idea (*any* idea, no matter how fuzzy) about your subject will help you identify the best possible materials right from the start and keep you from wasting time on unnecessary sources.
- *Ask yourself a few simple questions* about the play or performance (e.g., what you think it is about, what you like or don't like about it, how you think it achieves its effects) and sketch out preliminary answers to help you get started.
- *Maintain an open mind.* Often in the course of doing research, something will surface that makes you rethink your original position. Stay flexible in your thinking as you discover fresh ideas and perspectives.
- *Keep track of your materials by taking good notes.* This is not to say that you need to write copiously on every single source, but do follow through on those sources that seem especially fruitful, especially if your own ideas start "flowing" as you read, watch, or experience your source. Write down what you are thinking and note your sources (titles, authors, page numbers) as you do so. When

watching a performance, it may be preferable to jot down your thoughts quickly afterward (before your ideas get cold) than to take notes during it if you find that this distracts you from the experience of being a spectator.

- *Be discriminating.* Not everything having to do with your subject is going to be equally helpful. The good researcher finds ways of economically sorting through materials, retaining the most pertinent ones for her or his topic, and quickly moving on from those that are not useful. When researching books, scan the table of contents for chapter titles that seem pertinent and choose a key word or two to look for in the index. If there is nothing that relates to your area, move on to something else. Scanning footnotes and titles in journals is another quick way to check for pertinent material. Reading introductory and concluding paragraphs also is an effective way of quickly getting the gist of a book, chapter, or article.

- *Develop your own technique.* Everyone finds his or her own rhythm when researching. Some prefer to read and reread plays and primary sources, refining their own ideas quite a bit before looking at secondary materials. Others prefer to dive into all the secondary materials they can get their hands on as they develop their ideas, and many writers fall somewhere in between. The important thing is to conduct your research as efficiently as possible and to remain flexible in your own thinking as you are exposed to other ideas and opinions. For example, a student might be intimidated and overwhelmed when researching a famous playwright such as Anton Chekhov because of the large numbers of books, essays, and criticism that his work has engendered. If, however, that student decides that what he or she likes about Chekhov's plays is the way the action occurs amidst groups of people mingling and talking in a "living room" atmosphere, a way into the research has already been found. Focusing on "domestic interiors in Chekhov's later plays," for example, is a manageable place to start research. Remember that smaller, more focused topics are always better than broad general ones and that your own interests are the best source of ideas.

TYPES OF THEATRE RESEARCH

Finding the necessary information for an essay about theatre requires various types of research. The following are the kinds of resources, publications, and documents that can help you find the information you need, depending on your approach to your topic.

Textbooks

General history textbooks, or basic theatre history textbooks, are useful for obtaining the basic facts of the period under investigation. Remember to consult the bibliographies, works cited, or suggested reading lists at either the end of the text or the end of individual sections or chapters for help in starting your research on your topic. Specifically, the following list is a sampling of good sources that cover a range of periods and theatre cultures:

> Brown, John Russell. *The Oxford Illustrated History of Theatre*. Oxford: Oxford University Press, 1997.
>
> Greenwald, Michael. *The Longman's Anthology of Drama and Theatre: A Global Perspective*. New York: Longman, 2001.
>
> Jacobus, Lee. *The Bedford Introduction to Drama*. New York: Bedford/St. Martin's Press, 2000.
>
> Klaus, Carl. *Stages of Drama: Classical to Contemporary Theatre*. New York: St. Martin's Press, 1999.
>
> Nagler, A. M. *A Sourcebook of Theatrical History*. New York: Theatre Annual, 1952.
>
> Watson, Jack, and Grant Mckernie. *A Cultural History of Theatre*. New York: Longman, 1993.
>
> Wilmeth, Don, and Christopher Bigsby, eds. *The Cambridge History of American Theatre: Vol. 1. Beginnings to 1870*. Cambridge: Cambridge University Press, 1998.

Biographies, Autobiographies, Memoirs

The memoirs of actors, playwrights, directors, and others may contain important or interesting anecdotes or information, and so do biographies. For example, *Laurence Olivier* by Francis Beckett contains excerpts from Olivier's own memoirs about his early days as an actor and offers a historical overview of his generation of theatre artists.

Prefaces and Author's Notes

These are included in most written editions of plays and can contain the author's notions about when, why, or how the play was written or his or her ideas about its meaning to the world of the audience. Some authors, such as George Bernard Shaw, are as famous for their prefaces as they are for their plays. For example, *Prefaces to English Nineteenth Century Theatre* by Michael Booth offers analyses and excerpts of prefaces to English dramas, comedies, farces, pantomimes, extravaganzas, and burlesques of that time.

Performance Documents

Playbills, mission statements from theatre companies, dramaturge's or director's notes (often included with the playbill handed out as you enter the theatre), and statistics on ticket and subscription sales (the business office is the best place to obtain this kind of information) can be useful in your analysis. Some of the larger theatres maintain their own archives of this and other kinds of information. For example, the Wilma Theatre, a major regional theatre in Philadelphia, declares in its mission statement that it wishes to "represent a range of voices, viewpoints and production styles."[4] This information could be useful if you were to write about this particular theatre's artistic or political profile in its community.

Reviews

Reviews of productions are often helpful in determining the audience's initial reaction to the play. Reviewers note the comments and reactions of the audience in their reviews, and often their own attitudes tell you much about the period in which they write. For example, in 1802, Washington Irving wrote of his visit to the gallery at the First Park Theater, "The noise in this part of the house is somewhat similar to that which prevailed in Noah's ark; for we have an imitation of the whistles and yells of every kind of animal."[5]

---

[4]Zizka, Blanka and Jiri. "The Wilma Theatre's Mission Statement," *Playbill* (Philadelphia, 2005).
[5]Irving, Washington. "The Audience of the First Park Theater," in *A Sourcebook in Theatrical History*, ed. Ed Nagler (Toronto: Dover Books, 1952), 525.

Television, Magazines, and Newspaper Reports

Documentaries, interviews, special feature articles, and advertisements in the media are good sources of material. For example, the 1998 musical *Capeman* received a great deal of media coverage because of protesters who picketed the Broadway show each night. Examining this material could give you a good idea of how this production interfaced with the culture and community surrounding it. In another example, Mel Gussow's book *Conversations with Stoppard* contains multiple interviews with the playwright Tom Stoppard in which he discusses various plays, productions, and ideas.

Photographs, Museums, and Libraries

Look for special exhibits on the time period you wish to focus on or for information related to the theatergoing public (its rituals, dress, attitudes) of the time as it is included in an overall cultural portrait. Certain libraries are devoted to theatrical materials. For example, at the Billy Rose Theatre Collection at the New York Public Library for the Performing Arts, a user can

> examine a 1767 program for a performance of *Romeo and Juliet* in Philadelphia, study Edwin Booth's letters to his daughter, review the working script for Orson Welles's African-American *Macbeth*, study costume designs from the film *Anna and the King of Siam*, analyze a videotape of *A Chorus Line*, or read scripts from current television hits.[6]

Other kinds of research materials help you write an analysis of a play's form and content, such as a play's plot structure, its themes, or its symbols. Reading the work of other critics on your subject can help crystallize what it is you wish to say about it. Methodologies of acting, playwriting, and directing can help focus your arguments concerning the internal structures at work. Even consulting a list of definitions for language terms can aid the writer of this kind of essay by helping isolate specific rhetorical strategies at work in a playwright's (or critic's) use of language. Such terms as irony, paradox, comedy, allegory, aside, tragedy, tragicomedy, farce, parody, monologue, dialogue, epilogue,

---

[6]"About the Theater Collection," New York Public Library home page, <http://www.nypl.org/research/lpa/the/theabout.html>.

and many other terms help the writer identify specific techniques of playwriting. Recognizing and accurately identifying particular writing techniques lends the critical essay rhetorical power and credibility. The following titles may be useful for the student writing a close analysis of a play's structure and content:

Atlantic Theatre Company. *A Practical Handbook for the Actor*. New York: Vintage Books, 1986.

Ball, David. *Backwards and Forwards: A Technical Manual for Reading Plays*. Chicago: Southern Illinois University Press, 1998.

Benedetti, Robert. *Actor at Work*. New York: Allyn & Bacon, 2000.

Benedetti, Robert. *Director at Work*. New York: Prentice Hall, 1998.

Grote, David. *Script Analysis: Reading and Understanding the Playscript for Production*. Philadelphia: Wadsworth, 1984.

Hodge, Francis. *Play Directing: Analysis, Communication, and Style*. New York: Allyn & Bacon, 1999.

Ingham, Rosemary. *From Page to Stage: How Theatre Designers Make Connections between Scripts and Images*. Portsmouth, Me.: Heinemann Drama, 1998.

Moore, Sonia. *The Stanislavski System*. New York: Penguin Books, 1965.

Stanislavski, Constantin. *An Actor Prepares*. Translated by Elizabeth Reynolds Hapgood. New York: Routledge, 2003.

Thomas, James. *Script Analysis for Actors, Directors, and Designers*. Woburn, Mass.: Focal Press, 2004.

Playwright's Notes

Prefaces, afterwords, and internal notations (such as stage directions) can be rich sources of information about the playwright's intentions regarding the content, theme, or the shape of the play. Although the author's opinion is not definitive (i.e., it's not the only opinion about the play that matters), quoting an author's statements about, for example, a gesture that accompanies a line or how an actor's voice should sound when delivering a certain speech can be useful evidence. Thus, August Wilson's stage direction in *Fences* that Troy "takes a long drink from the bottle" before Rose's line "You're gonna drink yourself to death"[7] could be an important part

---

[7]Wilson, August. *Fences*, in *The Wadsworth Anthology of Drama*, ed. William Worthen (Boston: Wadsworth, 2004), 1159.

of your argument if you are writing about a particular character, theme, or relationship in that play.

Introductions

Introductions are often written by scholars who identify the play's main themes or who offer information about the author or their intentions that do not appear elsewhere in the play. For example, in his introduction to *Sam Shepard, Seven Plays*, Richard Gilman claims, "Not many critics would dispute the proposition that Sam Shepard is our most interesting and exciting American playwright."[8] Whether you agree or disagree, if you are writing about Shepard, this critical position could help you define your own argument.

Theatre Guides or Dictionaries

As noted above, a good comprehensive theatre dictionary or guide can be extremely useful, especially when looking up a specific play or playwright. The following texts are designed to have concise, comprehensive descriptions of plays and information about themes and techniques:

> Kennedy, Dennis. *The Oxford Encyclopedia of Theatre and Performance*. Oxford: Oxford University Press, 2003.
>
> Law, Jonathan. *The Penguin Dictionary of the Theatre*. New York: Penguin Books, 2001.
>
> Magill, Frank N. *Masterplots*. Salem: Salem Press, 1976.
>
> McLeish, Kenneth. *A Guide to Greek Theatre and Drama*. London: Methuen, 2003.
>
> Patterson, Michael. *The Oxford Dictionary of Plays*. Oxford: Oxford University Press, 2005.
>
> Sternlicht, Sanford. *A Reader's Guide to Modern British Drama*. Syracuse, N.Y.: Syracuse University Press, 2004.
>
> Unwin, Stephen, and Carole Woddis. *A Pocket Guide to 20th Century Drama*. New York: Faber and Faber, 2001.
>
> West, William N. *Theatres and Encyclopedias in Early Modern Europe*. Cambridge: Cambridge University Press, 2002.

[8]Gilman, Richard. "Introduction," in *Sam Shepard, Seven Plays* (Toronto: Bantam Books, 1981), ix.

FINDING ARTICLES, REVIEWS, CRITICISM, AND SCHOLARSHIP

Online databases and indexes can help you locate materials for all kinds of theatre essays quickly and easily. Many of the best general electronic database systems for theatre writers, including the *MLA International Bibliography*, *The Oxford Encyclopedia of Theatre and Performance*, and the *World Shakespeare Bibliography Online*, are available at most college and university libraries. The best online sources for past, present, and international theatre reviews are the *New York Times Theatre Reviews* and the *Readers' Guide to Periodical Literature*, which are also widely available through library systems. Additionally, there are hard copies of multiple theatre guides, dictionaries, and encyclopedias in most libraries' reference sections, and again, looking through their indexes for mention of a name or a key word in your topic is a good way to start gathering materials and information.

Indexes and Guides

Guides and indexes, both in print and online, help you find criticism and other articles on your topic. The *MLA International Bibliography*, for example, lists the scholarship on any given topic in a given year. It is published in hard copy but also as a CD-ROM and is available in many college and university libraries as part of their online research resources. Entering *MLA* in a library catalog key word or title search will get you there in most cases.

How to Use an Online Index

Let's say you are researching feminism and *A Doll's House* for your paper topic. You could use the MLA index to find an article you need by **typing MLA in the search engine of your library's home page** (sometimes there are "shortcuts" on this page, such as a box labeled "findit!"). You would then **use key words** to help refine your search to just those articles that would be pertinent to your topic. Once on the database's search screen, you could use the key words "Ibsen" and "A Doll's House" and "Feminis°" in the default fields. (Note that the ° in "Feminis" serves to truncate the root, so all words beginning with Feminis will be retrieved—feminist, feminism, and so on.) This search recently pulled up 11 items in a university library. Perhaps one of these articles is the one you need? To actually get the article, once you find it, click on the "Text" button next to the record. This will search other databases and e-journals in the library for an online copy. If no online copy is available, you may search the library's catalog for a print copy. Scanning article titles carefully will usually give you a good idea of their potential usefulness. If none of the articles you retrieve is useful, experiment with other key words. If searching MLA does not give you the article you need, you could try other databases or indexes with the same keywords or stay with the MLA index and experiment with other keywords.

To narrow down your research, limit your search to the last five years of research. Otherwise, you may be overwhelmed with information. Another useful, widely available online index is the *Readers' Guide to Periodical Literature*, which includes a wide variety of popular magazines. If, for example, you wanted to write a paper about the reception of a particular production of *A Doll's House*, you could find scholarly criticism of the production through the *MLA* index and reviews in popular magazines like *Newsweek* or *Time Magazine* through the *Readers' Guide to Periodical Literature*. Online indexes are updated more frequently than indexes in books, although some students and other researchers find the hard copies on the library shelves easier to use. The following online indexes could be very useful in helping you locate relevant articles and books for your research:

Academic Search Premier (EBSCO)
Full-text coverage of over 1,000 academic journals in a variety of disciplines from 1990 on, plus an index to thousands more dating from 1984.

Art Abstracts and Art Index Retrospective
Includes British and American art publications of all kinds, a good source for interviews with theatre practitioners.

Arts & Humanities Citation Index
Broadly interdisciplinary and international, covering articles from 1975 on.

Humanities Abstracts Full Text
Interdisciplinary index and abstracts in a number of fields, including drama and criticism.

International Bibliography of Theatre
Excellent resource specifically for theatre and performance, indexing major theatre periodicals and books from 1982 on.

International Index to the Performing Arts
Indexes documents on all aspects of performance, including profiles and discographies.

International Index to Periodicals
A list of theatre reviews is available in each annual volume. Look under "Drama," "Criticism," and "Plots."

Marks, Patricia. *American Literary and Drama Reviews: An Index to Late Nineteenth Century Periodicals*. Boston: G. K. Hall, 1984. Includes reviews of foreign plays from this period.

MLA Bibliography. New York: Modern Language Association of American, 1921–.
An index for criticism in related areas of study, including some unpublished works.

New York Theatre Critics' Reviews
Includes reviews from all major New York newspapers (some now defunct) from the years 1940–1994.

New York Times Directory of the Theater
An index to reviews from 1920 to 1970, plus a record of major theatre awards during those years.

New York Times Theater Reviews
One of the best resources for American theatre reviews from 1870 on. Contains reprinted articles as they originally appeared in the newspaper.

Readers' Guide to Periodical Literature
Broad-ranging database of articles in periodicals. Search under "Drama."

Salem, James. *A Guide to Critical Reviews*. Metuchen, N.J.: Scarecrow Press, 1971. This guide contains three volumes of particular use to the theatre writer: *American Drama, 1909–1982, Foreign Drama, 1909–1977,* and *The Musical, 1909–1989.*

Samples, Gordon. *How to Locate Reviews of Plays and Films: A Bibliography of Criticism from the Beginnings to the Present*. Metuchen, N.J.: Scarecrow Press, 1976.

Journals and Other Periodicals

Perhaps the best way to stay informed about the most recent trends in theatre research is to consult one of the journals or other periodicals that deal specifically in theatre research. Academic journals contain juried articles, that is, articles that have been reviewed and judged by the author's scholarly peers. They represent the newest research and thinking about a variety of academic approaches to theatre. The following is a partial list of key academic theatre journals:

New England Theatre Journal

PAJ: A Journal of Performance and Art

Shakespeare Quarterly

TDR; originally the Tulane Drama Review

Theatre and Event

Theatre History Studies

Theatre Journal

Theatre Topics

More commercial journals and magazines, such as *American Theatre Magazine, Curtain Up, Backstage, New York Theatre Experience, Scene4, The Stage, Stage Directions, Theater Magazine,* and *Variety* offer more informal (but often equally useful) articles about contemporary practitioners and trends in commercial and regional theatre.

✔ *A Checklist for Using Research Materials and Methods*

❑   Have you discriminated among materials, gathering only those that are pertinent to your topic?

❑   Does your research focus mainly on primary materials, emphasizing your own thinking and ideas?

❑   Are your Internet sources reliable and up to date?

❑   Have you considered what type of research is most appropriate for your topic?

❑   Have you kept an open mind about your research materials?

ORGANIZING RESEARCH

Losing track of your sources is one of the most common ways of losing valuable time when handling research. Once you have done research on primary and secondary sources, organizing your notes efficiently facilitates the writing process. Research is most helpful when it is readily available and clearly labeled. The following are tips for organizing research to best facilitate the writing process:

- *Organize information* by recording *complete bibliographical information* (including the author's name, book/article title, publishing information, and page numbers) as well as the author's ideas and opinions that are germane to your topic (in your own words) on note cards. Taking notes on your computer is of course also an option: for example, there is a "Notebook Layout" for taking notes under Microsoft Word. To access it in Microsoft Word, click on View>Notebook Layout. Notebook Layout is still just typing, however. To take notes with pictures—drawing graphs or figures—you'd need a notebook computer with a stylus for input. Note: Be sure to record complete bibliographic information for online sources as well as for print sources.
- *Check all quotations for accuracy.* Look back at your sources and make sure of both the wording and the page number of the quotation.
- *Arrange notes in a fashion that makes sense to you.* Whether this means organizing it chronologically, alphabetically by author or title, by theme, or according to some other system, this allows you to rapidly access the research during the writing process.

INCORPORATING RESEARCH

Your research will be integrated into your argument so that it helps sway the reader to your point of view. However, relying too much on the thinking of others takes away from the force of your own perspective, and using too many quotes (or using quotes that are too long) can dilute the very point you are trying to support. Thus, integrating your research judiciously can make all the difference in the persuasiveness of your argument.

Research assignments vary in length: evaluate how much and what kind of research would be appropriate for a given assignment. When your notes are organized and your preliminary outline is completed, you are ready to begin the first draft. As you write the first draft, allow your ideas to continue to evolve and make sure to use only those quotes and arguments from your research that directly support your own ideas. Learn to *summarize* the arguments of others, that is, to restate them succinctly without quoting or rehashing them at great length, using only those aspects of them that are most pertinent to your argument. However, especially when paraphrasing the work of other authors, it is important to avoid *plagiarizing*, that is, presenting the ideas of others as your own, by using proper citation to identify the authors and works whose ideas you are using (see the section "Avoiding Plagiarism" later in this chapter). Too many quotations are worse than none; they can confuse, dilute, or substitute for your argument about the subject. Following are some tips on integrating research into your argument effectively:

- *Choose carefully which ideas to summarize* and which to convey with a direct quotation. When summarizing an idea from a text, be sure to attribute the idea to the author from which it came. For example, "According to Frank Lord, Hamlet is Shakespeare's most existential hero."
- *Use an ellipsis* (. . .) if you wish to use part but not all of a quotation to indicate omissions. To use the previous sentence as an example, "Use an ellipsis . . . to indicate omissions."
- *Introduce quotations* by using transitional phrases between your own writing to the thinking of others. For example, "As Tom Stoppard puts it . . .", "According to Caryl Churchill . . .", and "In the words of Tennessee Williams . . ."
- *Avoid repetition* when using quotations. Let the quotation state the idea for you and use it as a springboard for your own thinking. Here is an example of an ineffective use of a quotation; it merely repeats something that the writer has already stated another way:

> Of all Shakespeare's characters, Hamlet is the most thoughtful about existential issues of life and death. As

> Frank Lord put it, "Hamlet is Shakespeare's most
> existential hero."

A better use of the quotation would be as follows:

> Frank Lord's remark that "Hamlet is Shakespeare's most
> existential hero" supports my argument that Hamlet has
> more in common with Hamm in Samuel Becket's
> *Endgame* than just the first syllable of his name.

Avoiding Plagiarism

The essay is *your* essay, not merely a rehash of what a dozen other people have said. Quotations, summaries, and paraphrases should not dominate the paper. Relying too much on the opinions of others weakens the integrity and interest of your argument and runs the risk of plagiarism. Plagiarism consists of taking credit for the work of others. You can avoid it by making sure that your ideas and point of view emerge as the dominant voice and that you acknowledge all outside voices and opinions as such. You can do this during the process of redrafting by doing the following:

- *Emphasizing your primary sources* over your secondary sources, that is, your own experience and opinion of primary texts and performances over the interpretation of those texts and performances by others
- *Clarifying where your research appears in the draft* by marking it with a colored pen; identify your *own ideas* with a different color and check to make sure your ideas appear more often in the paper

Develop a sense of what can be considered common knowledge: for instance, the fact that Hamlet is an indecisive character is common knowledge and does not need to be credited to any particular book or writer. Likewise, the date of Shakespeare's birth and the date that Hamlet was written are facts that are so widely available elsewhere that they do not need documentation. However, David Bevington's interesting observation that "Hamlet, for his part, is so obsessed with the secret murder that he overreacts to those around him" could not be considered common knowledge. The following example of plagiarism paraphrases this passage without crediting Bevington: "Hamlet is so preoccupied by his father's murder that he overacts to everyone around him." A more radical rewording of Bevington's basic idea is still unacceptable: "Hamlet lashes out at his friends and family because he is consumed by the murder." This kind of paraphrasing is appropriate only when the author is specifically acknowledged:

> There is a real reason for Hamlet's "madness." As Bevington put it, Hamlet is "so obsessed with the secret murder" that he lashes out at his friends and family. (899)

Using another writer's ideas can be helpful in expressing your own arguments, as long as you acknowledge their work. Always acknowledge and credit your sources when you are

- borrowing or quoting specific words and/or phrases,
- using others' ideas, or
- paraphrasing material.

✔ A Checklist for Organizing and Incorporating Research

❑   Are your notes organized in an easily accessible form?

❑   Do all your notes contain accurate bibliographical information, including author, title, date and place of publication, and page numbers?

❑   Have you checked all quotations for accuracy?

❑   Does your research support your own ideas, or does your thinking rely too much on the ideas of others?

❑   Have you avoided the possibility of plagiarism by carefully acknowledging and crediting all your sources?

How to Document Research Sources: Formatting Citations in MLA Style

Always use the proper method of citation for your sources, according to your instructor's preferences. The usual default convention is to use the MLA (Modern Languages Association) style of formatting citations when no other specific style is mandated. Footnotes have generally fallen out of favor. Currently, a **parenthetical citation** and a **Works Cited** list at the end of the essay is the preferred form of documenting your sources:

> Marsha Norman's protagonist in her 1983 play 'Night, Mother is honest and brutal to her mother when explaining her decision to commit suicide: "What if the only way I can get away from you for good is to kill myself? What if it is? I can *still* do it!" (72).

The reference, of course, is to 'Night, Mother, but notice that only the page number is provided in parentheses after the quotation, with the final punctuation after the parenthetical citation. The rest of the bibliographical information, such as publisher, date, and place of publication, can be found at the end of the essay in the Works Cited list.

Here the writer mentions the author's name and the name of the play within the essay itself, but if you do not provide such information, you must supply it in the parentheses, before the page number, with the name and number separated by a comma. For example, for the quotation above the citation would be: (Norman, 'Night, Mother, 72). The reader can then turn to Works Cited, find the author's name (names are listed alphabetically, last names first), and know where to go if for some reason he or she wishes to check the quotation. When quoting from a classical play or a play with divisions and numbered lines, instead of referring to page numbers, your instructor may prefer that you cite quoted lines by division and line numbers. In this case, separate the act from the scene and the scene from the line by periods and use Arabic (not Roman) numerals in the following order: act, scene, and line number(s). For example, the quotation used below is taken from act 3, scene 4, lines 88 to 89:

> The motif of sight and its potential for harm is echoed in Queen Gertrude's lines, "O Hamlet, speak no more:/Thou turn'st mine eyes into my very soul." (3. 4. 88–89)

A Works Cited list at the end of the essay provides further details about the play's publication. This list is arranged in alphabetical order according to the author's last name (last name first), so that the reader can easily look up the author's name to find the source of the quote. In the Works Cited list, the author's name, the full title, and the place and date of publication are given in the following manner:

> Norman, Marsha. 'Night, Mother. New York: Hill and Wang, 1983.

In a research paper on theatre, you may use many different kinds of sources. The following sampling provides MLA style formats for many, but not all, kinds of material you may encounter when writing a paper about theatre. Most libraries have the *MLA Style Manual* available as a reference work, and reference librarians are also a great resource for questions about citation and documentation that do not appear here.

Print Sources

Books and Published Plays

Churchill, Caryl. *Cloud 9*. New York: Routledge, 1984.

Edition of a Book or Play

Shakespeare, William. *Hamlet*. Ed. Barbara A. Mowat and Paul Westine. New York: Washington Square/Pocket, 1992.

(Note that turnover lines in MLA citations are indented five spaces, that citations are single spaced with double spaces between entries, and that the title "Ed." is given to the editors.)

Article or Essay within a Book

States, Bert. "The Phenomenological Attitude." *Critical Theory and Performance*. Ed. Janelle Reinelt and Joseph Roach. Ann Arbor: University of Michigan Press, 1992.

Journal and Magazine Articles

Barth, Diana. "London Theatre: Highlights of the Fall Season." *Western European Stages*. Volume 8. Number 2, (Spring 1996): 17–22.

Review from Print Newspaper

Collins, William. "A Multimedia '1984' at Wilma Theater." *Philadelphia Inquirer*, 7 May 1986: sec. D, 1.

Preface, Foreword, Afterword, or Introduction

Cowan, Suzanne. Foreword. *Orgasmo Adulto Escapes from the Zoo*. By Franca Rame and Dario Fo. New York: Broadway Play Publishing, 1985.

Multimedia and Live Performance Sources

Much Ado about Nothing. By William Shakespeare. Dir. David Esbjornson. Delacorte Theater, New York. 7 Aug. 2004.

Individual Performance

Streep, Meryl, perf. *The Seagull.* By Anton Chekhov. Dir. Mike Nichols. Delacorte Theater, New York. 25 July 2001.

Interview

Messmer, Lydia. Interview with Mark W. Allem. *Interview with Lydia Messmer: Oral History.* 1987. Videotape. University Archives, U. of Pennsylvania.

Television/Radio Program

American Experience. WHYY. 29 May 2006.

Lecture

Fava, Antonio. Lecture. University of Pennsylvania. 7 February 2006.

Electronic Sources

Article from Online Magazine

Windman, Matt. "Playbill.com's Brief Encounter with Eric Schaeffer." *Playbill.com.* 19 Jun 2006 <http://www.playbill.com/celebritybuzz/article/100402. html>.

Article from Online Newspaper

Gates, Anita. "Brainy Black Women, Still Looking for Love, in 'Single Black Female'." 20 June 06, *New York Times.* 20 June 2006 <http://theater2.nytimes.com/2006/06/20/theater/reviews/20fema.html>.

Article from Full-Text Database

Gourevitch, Victor. "Rousseau on Providence." *Review of Metaphysics* (March 2000). *Expanded Academic ASAP.* Detroit, Mich.: Gale Group; Philadelphia: University of Pennsylvania

Library, 2 December 2001. http://web7.infotrac.galegroup.com/
itw/infomark=upenn_main.

SAMPLE STUDENT ESSAYS

Here are two thoughtful essays about the same play, only the second of which is supported by research. Compare the resulting differences in rhetorical force (the ability to persuade the reader) between them and observe the way research is integrated into the argument. Research has not only supported the author's thinking; in addition, because of her research, her ideas have evolved and extended in important ways.

Harriet Nolan

Unsympathetic Sisters: Creating Empathy through the Use of Contrast and Ensemble in Chekhov's *The Three Sisters*

Opening paragraph informs reader of basic plotline and writer's attitude.

Anton Chekhov's 1901 play *The Three Sisters* depicts the unhappy life of aimless people. Through long monologues and conversations with the friends and relatives who surround them, we learn that the three sisters in question (Olga, Masha, and Irina) yearn for a past filled with wealth, social position, and a purpose now denied them. Since their father's death several years earlier, the sisters have been forced to move from their beloved city of Moscow to a smaller, provincial Russian town where they must live less glamorous lives. Their desire to return to Moscow becomes a constant motif in conversations among themselves and with others. Returning to this theme so constantly makes the sisters seem somewhat immature, even peevish. The audience understandably may tire of hearing this refrain, and even find the sisters annoying at times. There is very little real dramatic action in the play;

Good transition at end of paragraph: thesis stated in question form.

essentially the audience watches as the sisters struggle with disappointment about their present circumstances and regret over lost chances. How, then, does the playwright create empathy for this self-absorbed trio of sisters?

There is little in the way of suspense to keep the spectator wondering "what happens next," so instead our attention is focused on the characters themselves, their relationships, their beliefs, and the social world they create together. The genius of this playwright is that he presents these characters in all their flawed humanity, but it is precisely their own fallibility that ultimately makes the spectators care for these characters. I will argue in this paper that he does so through the use of two techniques in particular: contrast and ensemble scenes.

Through the use of contrast between a large variety of different types of characters (including doctors, soldiers, teachers, servants, spinsters, and married couples), and also through ensemble scenes that include them all simultaneously, Chekhov creates an onstage world of human variety in which all characters are fallible and flawed, but all ultimately win our hearts because of their quintessentially humanity. For example, in Act One the Protzoroz sisters at first seem snobbish, especially with regard to a local girl, Natasha, in whom their brother has recently shown a romantic interest. In the following speech, Masha describes Natasha in a condescending, nasty way that makes us feel sorry for Natasha and resentful of Masha's superiority:

*Good intro-
duction of
quotation:
calls our
attention to
elements of
quote that
are pertinent
to writer's
argument.*

> Masha: Oh, how she dresses! It's not that her
> clothes are simply ugly or outmoded, it's just that
> they turn out pathetic. Some sort of strange, bright-
> yellowish skirt, with a cheap vulgar fringe on it, and
> a red blouse. And her cheeks are scrubbed clean.
> My, how scrubbed they are! Andrey is not in
> love—I won't admit to that, he has taste, after all.
> It's simply that he's teasing us, he's playing the
> fool. (111)[9]

While Natasha at first engages the sympathies of the audience through her apparent social inferiority to the

[9]All page references given parenthetically within the essay refer to Anton Chekhov *The Three Sisters*, in *Anton Chekhov's Plays*, ed. Eugene Bristow (New York: Norton, 1977), 111.

sisters and her initial nervousness around them, Chekhov builds in a contrasting reality for this character and for the sisters that leads the audience to see them both in a very different light. Natasha does marry their brother, and over the course of the play she claims more and more power over the household, until by the end she pushes Olga out of the house and Irina out of her bedroom. In Act Three, Olga is seen comforting their old nursemaid Anfisa, who, at eighty years old, is feeling lonely and exhausted. In the next lines, Natasha enters the room and scolds first Anfisa and then Olga:

> Natasha: (*to Anfisa, coldly*) Don't you dare sit down in my presence! Get out! On your way now! (*Anfisa goes out; a pause*) And why on earth you hold onto that old woman I don't understand! . . . She has no purpose in being here! She is a peasant, she should live in the country. . . . I've never seen such mollycoddling! (134)

Chekhov uses contrast in three ways in this example. First, he shows us a contrast within Natasha's character before and after her marriage to their brother. Her changed status affects her behavior and allows her more ''vulgar'' qualities to come out. Second, whereas she was once their social inferior, now she wields more power than the sisters, and she uses it in cruel ways that make the sisters' pettishness seem comparatively minor faults by comparison. Third, the way the sisters treat Anfisa contrasts with the way Natasha does, which shows the sisters in a new light, as people who, while self-absorbed, are also capable of loyalty and empathy.

Use of numbers ("first," "second," and "third") orients and guides reader to main points.

Another example of Chekhov's use of contrast to create empathy in the audience lies in the relationships between servants and masters. While the masters, and the sisters in particular, spend most of their time bemoaning their fate and questioning their function in life, the servants by contrast are capable of enjoying life and regarding their employment as giving them meaning and purpose in life. This contrast also results in irony: the relatively lowly servants in the play have a distinct advantage over the sisters, who miserably search for a purposeful direction in their lives, even as they embody that purpose for the servants. For example, in the following lines, Anfisa rejoices in her new life with Olga, after both have been forcibly ejected from the household by Natasha:

> Anfisa: . . . Sinner that I am, I've never lived like
> this . . . the apartment big, paid for by the
> government, and for me a whole room and my own
> bed. All of it paid for by the government. I wake up
> in the night and—oh, dear Lord, Mother of God,
> never was there a happier person than me! (153)

By creating contrast through these servant characters, who are happy simply to have enough work to feed themselves, Chekhov shows another dimension to the Protzorov sisters, who on the one hand seem spoiled by their comforts (their education, culture, and status), and yet victimized by those same things, without which they subsequently cannot live happily. Here Chekhov again uses contrast to portray the sisters in all their intimate and contradictory detail, drawing the audience into having empathy for them by seeing them in all the flawed, multifaceted dimension of their humanity.

While the sisters' longing for their former life in Moscow may become tiresome to the audience, through the ensemble scenes Chekhov makes us see that the sisters are not alone in this attitude, that in fact they are surrounded by a whole community of people who vocally and communally grieve over the past. In fact, this company affirms their longing, justifying it by sharing reminiscences of their father, their parties, their lost lives. For example, in Act One Vershinin, a visiting Battery commander, recalls, ". . . Your father I have preserved in my memory; I have only to close my eyes to see him as though he were alive. I used to visit you in Moscow . . ." (109) The audience's annoyance is thus diffused, as they recognize that reminiscence in general is a *Specific detail from text supports and extends main thesis.* defining feature of the onstage world. By using these ensemble scenes, Chekhov contextualizes their desire for Moscow and an irretrievable lost life, making it seem more like a shared social condition than a singular obsession.

Conclusion adequately proved through well-organized argument and adequate evidence; conclusion restates but does not expand on opening thesis.

Chekhov invites us to see several sides to his characters: they are spoiled and annoying, brave and solitary, lonely and heroic, self-absorbed and loyal all at once. In short, they contain contrasting characteristics, just like real human beings. In conclusion, through the use of contrast and ensemble scenes, Chekhov permits us to relate to his characters the way we relate to our own families; we put up with their idiosyncrasies and annoying habits because we see beyond them, and are rewarded for this by loving them, too. Chekhov's play speaks directly to the audience, conveying its message about the destructive effects of purposelessness on the human spirit by making us empathize with these flawed, afflicted sisters.

This paper does a fine job of presenting a cohesive argument about Chekhov's use of two techniques, contrast and ensemble scenes, to create empathy in the audience for his somewhat difficult characters. It is fairly well organized and uses well-chosen quotations from the text to support this argument. However, it does not go beyond its initial thesis statement ("he does so through the use of two techniques in particular: contrast and ensemble scenes"), and its conclusion is basically a restatement of that thesis ("In conclusion, through the use of contrast and ensemble scenes, Chekhov permits us to relate to his characters"). The paper does not attempt to persuade the reader that there are any connections between Chekhov's play and other larger traditions, histories, or techniques. It is competent but not ambitious, and it relies entirely on the play itself to convince the reader of the validity of the writer's point of view. And here is the second essay, this one supported by research.

Carson Greenspan

Chekhov's *The Three Sisters*: Reflecting an Era, Inventing a Technique

Anton Chekhov's (1860–1904) plays have become staples of the Western canon, but they were not always considered the classics that they are today. In fact, when his first play, *The Seagull*, was first produced at the

Alexandrinsky Theatre in St. Petersburg in 1896, it was such a colossal failure that he almost decided to give up playwriting entirely. Luckily, the Moscow Art Theatre revived the play in a subsequent production, and its success encouraged him to write three more plays for the company, *Uncle Vanya* (1899), *The Three Sisters* (1901), and *The Cherry Orchard* (1904). Chekhov's genius lies in his invention of realistic playwriting techniques to accurately reflect the experiences of a certain social class, and to imbue that reflection with the dimensions of individual human experience, both comic and tragic. Although we now take the theatrical mode of realism for granted, Chekhov's realistic plays were so innovative for their time that new methods of acting and producing had to be invented just to stage them (Brockett, 488). This paper will look specifically at why Chekhov was drawn to this particular mode of writing, at how *The Three Sisters* in particular reflects a social reality of Chekhov's own place and era, and at the implications of Chekhov's innovations for our own time.

First paragraph states thesis, suggests its relevance.

Each of his major plays are set in provincial Russia, and "depict the monotonous and frustrating life of the landowning class" (Brockett, 487). This is a class of people who really existed in Chekhov's own time; a landed aristocracy who had outlived their milieu and were forced to adapt and find a different way of life. According to historian Ronald Hingley, in Imperial Russia at the end of the nineteenth century, "the gentry's importance in Russian culture is completely out of proportion to its numbers—just over one percent of the population" (222). It is this small portion of Russia's population that fascinated Anton Chekhov. He himself was the descendent of serfs, and he wrote stories at first to better support his family, because his job as a physician was relatively low paying. Chekhov, in other words, was not documenting his own class in turning to this small group of people for the subjects of his plays; he was instead documenting a vanishing breed of cultured Russians, who no longer had a specific function in the newly bourgeois world of late nineteenth-century Russia. As Chekhov critic Ralph Matlaw observes, he was "the voice of

Good use of historical evidence to flesh out background of topic.

Good use of critical secondary source to expand sociohistorical context of play.

Good transition: paragraphs building on each other.

twilight Russia" a scribe who conveyed the last stories of a dwindling class to the world.

For many of Chekhov's characters, the task of adapting to new ways of life proves impossible. They lack the initiative or the imagination to change, and remain in a kind of resigned fantasy world of their own making. The Protzorov family in *The Three Sisters* are perfect examples of this phenomenon; trapped by their current circumstances, they prefer to dream about their old life in Moscow than to do anything to really improve their lives in the province where they actually live. As Irina says, "I'm bored to death, there's nothing to do, and I hate the room where I live. . . . So I've decided once and for all that if it's not my fate to live in Moscow, then so be it. It's my fate, pure and simple, and you can't do anything about it" (147). Thus the play is really a meditation upon a certain state of mind, and rather than a *Restatement of theme, supported by quote.* plot full of dramatic action, external action and movement, Chekhov wrote a play that depicts a suspended, internal emotional state.

Perhaps Chekhov's biography gives us a clue as to his choice of style as a playwright, a choice that allowed him to dramatize this "internal" world of his characters. As a doctor, he was called upon to observe patients and diseases in a clinical and detached manner. Similarly, he presents his characters in all their contradictory nature for the audience to observe. Many playwrights of this era treated characters in conventional ways, imbuing them with consistent, easily recognizable traits that easily complemented or opposed one another, and pushed the dramatic action along familiar lines of conflict and reconciliation. Instead, as we see in *The Three Sisters*, Chekhov's characters contain numerous contradictory qualities: Masha is cruel to Natasha, but sensitive and *Use of bio- graphical detail further expands and deepens paper's reach.* vulnerable to others; Olga is sympathetic and comforting but also frustrated and exhausted; Irina is practically suicidal in her discontent but capable of reassuring her siblings when they are distressed. It is almost as if this doctor-turned-playwright does not want the audience to

Excellent use of letter to substantiate writer's argument about Chekhov's technique.

be too hasty in making up their minds about any of them. In one of his letters, Chekhov claims that "The artist should be, not the judge of his characters and their conversations, but only an unbiased witness" (Garnett, 88). The artist's relationship to society is not to dictate action or solutions, for Chekhov, but simply to present the complications and contradictions of "real" characters for the audience to contemplate and "diagnose."

Yet staging this kind of psychological realism challenged conventional methods of dramatic storytelling. This was a very different kind of play in its day, and it required new ways of thinking about theatre to make it come alive. The head of the Moscow Art Theatre at the time, the famed Constantin Stanislavski, invented a whole new system of acting, which privileged the reality of the character's emotional state over external gesture and recitation (the accepted mode of acting in that time), in order to realize these plays (Brockett, 466). According to W. B. Worthen, The Moscow Art Theatre's success in staging Chekhov's plays was due to "Stanislavski's commitment to a restrained style of performance, emphasizing sychological complexity and balanced playing by the entire ensemble . . ." (644). His innovations acknowledged the primacy of internal emotional

Secondary source amplifies and substantiates claim for play's importance to contemporary theatre.

states in acting, and were critical to the evolution of Western acting practices in general. Stanislavski's "method" was soon transformed into one of the most influential of all acting approaches. Perhaps its most famous American manifestation was the Actor's Studio, as headed by Lee Strasburg, although many other approaches and theorists are also indebted to Stanislavski's (and by association, Chekhov's) innovations.

We have seen how Chekhov's scientific orientation, as well as his own experiences in his own culture and history, led him to represent a certain social class of characters that fascinated and moved him by developing challenging plays that demanded new responses from both audiences and practitioners. Because of his insistence that the role of the artist was to present human life in all its complexity, audiences then and now are challenged to think for themselves. As Matlaw puts it, "Chekhov was not given to generalities . . . but rather insisted on honesty and truth, on depicting what existed *Conclusion* rather than what one hoped to see because one saw *does not just* in automatic, ordinary, and unthinking ways". This *restate thesis* insistence on dramatizing the reality of complex, inter- *but expands* nal emotions stimulated evolutions not only in the *on it to* audience, but also across many other facets of theatre, *include con-* from playwriting to acting, directing and producing. *sideration of* Contemporary theatres, readers, and audiences are *historical,* indebted to Chekhov's commitment to his own unique and *artistic impli-* scientific approach to his characters. *cations of the play.*

Works Cited

Brockett, Oscar. *History of the Theatre.* Boston: Allyn & Bacon, 1991. Sixth edition.

Chekhov, Anton. *Letters*, trans. Constance Garnett. New York: Kessinger Publishing, 2005.

Hingley, Ronald. "Chekhov's Russia," in *Anton Chekhov's Plays*, ed. Eugene Bristow. New York: Norton, 1977.

Matlaw, Ralph, ed. "Preface." *Anton Chekhov's Short Stories.* New York: Norton, 1979.

Worthen, W. B. *The Wadsworth Anthology of Drama.* Berkeley: University of California Press, 2007. Fifth edition.

Note that this paper, like the first one, offers a cohesive argument about Chekhov's techniques as a writer, but whereas the first paper stopped short of relating that technique to other things, this paper is far more ambitious. The writer uses research on Chekhov's life, on the history of Russia, and on other theatre practitioners (specifically Stanislavski) to connect the techniques at work in *The Three Sisters* to larger trends in history and art. His argument is particularly convincing because he successfully integrates his research into his paper. Although engaging a number of outside sources, he does not overuse quotations or make them redundant; instead, he carefully employs them to enhance his argument. This writer's conclusion summarizes the ways in which the play and playwright are important today ("Contemporary theatres, readers, and audiences are indebted to Chekhov's commitment to his own unique and scientific approach to his characters"). Research strengthens and persuades the reader of the truth of this conclusion and forms the basis for the paper's investigation into how the play and playwright *means* something to audiences. With a broader and more interesting scope, this student uses research effectively to help organize and support the essay's thesis.

6

THE CHARACTER/SCENE ANALYSIS

Thus the actor must be able to decide what is going on in the text in simple, actable terms.

—MELISSA BRUDER

Now that we have examined several types of theatre essays, including the review response, the production response, and the analytical essay, we will turn to another one: the character/scene analysis. We have chosen to locate our discussion of the character/scene analysis at the end of this book because it represents a distinctly different approach from the previously described essays. This type of writing is a functional tool used by actors and directors. The character/scene analysis asks writers to explain goals and methods in the performance of theatre, answering such fundamental questions as, How would an actor go about playing this role? and How would a director direct this scene? It is a practical document that is meant to clearly outline the student actor's or director's approach to the material of the play. Students learning any of the many crafts that make up theatre (such as acting, directing, or design) must also learn to create a kind of "blueprint" that shows or demonstrates exactly how that craft will work to create specific theatrical effects. The character/scene analysis is an example of such a document because it demonstrates how to break down or analyze a scene or character in order to act or direct it. Other examples include a designer's sketch for a costume, a lighting plot, or a director's ground plan (a sketch showing the placement of all elements of the stage picture, including set pieces, props, and the positions of the actor's bodies at a given moment in the play).

The character/scene analysis is commonly assigned in acting and directing classes. Its purpose is to present a convincing and useful interpretation of a specific scene or of a character within a scene. In a college course, the goal may also be to demonstrate to the instructor your knowledge of the vocabulary of acting or directing. This kind of assignment asks the student to perform a *script analysis*, that is, to break the play, scene, or character down into component parts that will then facilitate the acting and/or directing of it. An actor's or a director's analysis of a scene or role has very important implications for his or her overall interpretation of the play. For example, if an actor playing Blanche DuBois in the Tennessee Williams play *A Streetcar Named Desire* decides that her character is attracted to Stanley Kowalski from their first scene together, that decision will have a radical effect on the rest of the play, which centers on a struggle between those two characters. Writing a character/scene analysis helps the student articulate exactly when, where, and how those important interpretive decisions are implemented onstage.

SCRIPT VERSUS PLAY TEXT

A *script* is a "working version" of a play. An actor's, a designer's, or a director's script may be identical to the published text of the play, or it may reflect additions or deletions made in the process of staging their particular production of it. Some plays are legally protected from changes made by directors (such as those of playwright Samuel Becket), while others specifically invite a collaborative approach to the material (such as contemporary American playwright Charles Mee). We will refer to the text of the play as a *script* for the purposes of this chapter, which describes the process of transferring the written word to the living stage, because the word *script* connotes an evolving document that is marked up and manipulated by theatre artists as they breathe life into it by staging it.

As mentioned before, to *analyze* means to break down into component pieces, the better to understand the relation of the parts to the whole. In a *script analysis*, the actor or director "breaks down" the script into smaller sections or units in order to construct a workable and logical interpretation of the play. In a *scene analysis*, the scene is similarly broken down into sections called *beats* (rhythmic units within the scene) to determine what is happening within every beat. The scene is then "put back together," beat by beat, in such a way that it reflects decisions about how those individual moments contribute to the overall rhythm, pace, structure, and meaning of the scene as a whole. In a *character analysis*, the same thing happens, except the scene is examined from the point of view of one particular character within the scene. The analysis reveals the "spine" of the scene or character, that is, its essential *shape*. The basic idea is to determine what the characters *want or need* during any given moment of the play (known as their *objective*) and to decide what *actions* they will take to achieve that goal within the scene (and, eventually, over the course of the whole play). As Stanislavski once wrote, "Every objective must carry in itself the germ of action."

For example, read the following excerpts from the production notebook of Elia Kazan, famous American director of the first (and extremely successful) Broadway production of Tennessee Williams's *A Streetcar Named Desire*. Here Kazan breaks two characters down to what he feels are their most essential qualities and needs. These are his character analyses for the two male leads in that play, first Stanley and then Mitch (see Figure 6a).

Sample Professional Character/Scene Analysis

Stanley is deeply indifferent. When he first meets Blanche he doesn't really seem to care if she stays or not. Stanley is interested in his own pleasures. He is completely self-absorbed to the point of fascination. To physicalize this: he has a most annoying way of being preoccupied—or of busying himself with something else when people are talking with him, at him it becomes. Example, first couple of pages Scene 2.[1]

MITCH—spine—to get away from his mother (Blanche the lever). . . . He doesn't want to be Mother's Boy. Goddamn it he just can't help it. Blanche makes a man out of him, makes him important and

---

[1]Elia Kazan, "Notebook for *A Streetcar Named Desire*," in *Directors on Directing*. ed. Toby Col and Helen Chinoy (New York: Bobbs-Merrill, 1963), 376.

Figure 6a. Marlon Brando as Stanley Kowalski in the original Broadway production of *A Streetcar Named Desire*.

Photo from author's collection.

grown-up. His Mother-he dimly realizes-keeps him eternally ado-lescent, forever dependent.[2]

These excerpts show Kazan breaking down and analyzing the script to discover their essential or defining characteristics—for Mitch it is his dependence on his mother, for Stanley it is his self-absorption. These decisions show how Kazan used the principles behind a character/scene analysis to document (and direct) his interpretation of this play.

Playing a role or directing a scene has been described in various ways: it has been compared to carving a turkey, sailing a boat down a channel, or (like Frankenstein) bringing human material to

---

[2]Kazan, "Notebook for *A Streetcar Named Desire*," 378.

life. No matter what language is used to describe it, the challenge is the same: living truthfully in the imaginary moment to create a believable character. Yet even the most talented actors and directors cannot rely on sheer artistic inspiration alone to see them through this complicated process. They need a reliable technique to give them a rock-solid foundation should inspiration fail them.

Stanislavski's Techniques

Influential Russian actor, director, and theorist Constantin Stanislavski (1863–1938) developed a technique to provide just such a foundation, one that is still in use today in most Western acting and directing training programs. Although Stanislavski's name may not be familiar to you, his groundbreaking acting theory continues to inform most contemporary American script analysis and acting technique. Stanislavski broke with the traditional forms of acting that were popular in his time, which relied mainly on external technique, featuring predetermined poses, gestures, and set vocal patterns. He instead claimed the potential for "internal belief" or authentic emotion in the actor and developed a set of theories and exercises designed to help the actor access such belief and emotion at will. Stanislavski's principles provide the concepts and vocabulary for the character/scene analysis, which in turn provides the actor and/or director with a document to help "map" one's work. Although some of the terms may change from school to school (e.g., an "objective" can also be called a "motivation" or a "justification," an "action" may also be called a "tactic," and a "tool" may be termed a "strategy"), the basic approach remains the same. Your instructors will teach their own versions of these terms, and they are the ones you should use in your essay. The key terms of the character/scene analysis are

- beats,
- objectives,
- actions,
- obstacles,
- transitions, and
- climax or turning point.

Finding these elements reveals the interpretive "arc of action" behind the performance or direction of a script, in addition to identifying the "given circumstances" of the play's basic situation. All are essential to understanding the scene's underlying structure.

Below is a working example of the process of writing a character/ scene analysis. Our working example is the sleepwalking scene from Shakespeare's *Macbeth* (see Figure 6b). It is a good choice for the character/scene analysis because Lady Macbeth is speaking her conscience in her sleep, unaware of her interlocutors (people listening), the Doctor and the Waiting Gentlewoman. For this reason she is speaking truthfully about her anxiety over the murders that she and her husband have committed, and the underlying motivations behind her behavior are brought out into the open. The first step is to read the scene carefully and identify the Stanislavskian

Figure 6b. The sleepwalking scene: Betty Miller as Lady Macbeth in the 1962 New York Shakespeare Festival production of *Macbeth*.

Photo credit: Photofest, Inc.

elements listed as the **primary elements** of the character/scene analysis. This kind of "detective work" is the best research for the character/scene analysis, and once firm answers have been reached, the writer is ready to make the choices that will shape his or her interpretation.

Sample Scene

LADY MACBETH: Yet here's a spot.

DOCTOR: Hark, she speaks: I will set down what comes from her, to satisfy my remembrance the more strongly.

LADY MACBETH: Out, damned spot; out, I say. One: two,— why, then 'tis time to do't. Hell is murky. Fie, my lord, fie, as soldier, and afeard? What need we fear who knows it when none can call our power to account? Yet who would have thought the old man to have had so much blood in him.

DOCTOR: Do you mark that?

LADY MACBETH: The Thane of Fife had a wife. Where is she now? What, will these hands ne'er be clean? No more o' that, my lord, no more o' that. You mar all with this starting.

DOCTOR: Go to, go to. You have known what you should not.

GENTLEWOMAN: She has spoke what she should not, I am sure of that. Heaven knows what she has known.

LADY MACBETH: Here's the smell of the blood still. All the perfumes of Arabia will not sweeten this little hand. O, O, O!

DOCTOR: What a sigh is there! The heart is sorely charged.

GENTLEWOMAN: I would not have such a heart in my bosom for the dignity of the whole body.

DOCTOR: Well, well, well.

GENTLEWOMAN: Pray God it be, sir.

DOCTOR: This disease is beyond my practice. Yet I have known those which have walked in their sleep who have died holily in their beds.

LADY MACBETH: Wash your hands, put on your nightgown, look not so pale. I tell you yet again, Banquo's buried. He cannot come out on's grave.

DOCTOR: Even so?

LADY MACBETH: To bed, to bed. There's knocking at the gate. Come, come, come, come, give me your hand. What's done cannot be undone. To bed, to bed, to bed.[3]

PRIMARY ELEMENTS OF A CHARACTER/SCENE ANALYSIS

Given Circumstances

Given circumstances are the essential facts shaping the character or scene under consideration. In writing the character/scene analysis, you must discover and record everything you can about these circumstances. They are to be found everywhere in the text: in the stage directions, in the dialogue, sometimes even within the title of the play. The following are the essential **given circumstances** of the sleepwalking scene from *Macbeth*:

- *Geographical location:* We are told in stage directions that the sleepwalking scene takes place in an anteroom in the castle at Dunsinane, which is located in Scotland.
- *Date:* It is nighttime. We are not given a specific time period or season; however, there is much thunder and lightening (especially in the scenes with the witches), so we can at least deduce that it is not an especially sunny or pleasant time of year.
- *Economic environment:* Macbeth has a castle and servants and entertains on a grand scale. Lady Macbeth is attended by at least one Gentlewoman. They host a banquet in the previous scene. All these details (and many more) tell us much about their economic situation.
- *Religious environment:* Lady Macbeth refers to hell ("hell is murky") and the Gentlewoman to heaven ("heaven knows

---

[3]William Shakespeare, *Macbeth*, in *The Norton Shakespeare*, ed. Stephen Greenblatt et al. (New York: Norton, 1997), 2609.

what she has known") during this scene. The notion of spiritual evil pervades the entire play, and the actor or director writing this character/scene analysis would have to make interpretive decisions about how strongly the religious environment affects the scene.

- *Political environment:* Lady Macbeth has committed herself to a plot to ensure that her husband ascends the throne of Scotland. The murders that torment her dreams in this scene are a result of this political situation. You could also look at the relationship between Lady Macbeth and her Gentlewoman as a political aspect of the scene (as employer and employee), and there are certainly many other political dimensions to the play as a whole.

- *Social environment:* The same relationship cited in the political environment (Lady Macbeth and the Gentlewoman) has bearing on the social environment of the scene, an example of how elements of the given circumstances may overlap two or more categories. That her social inferiors (the Doctor and the Gentlewoman) are secretly observing Lady Macbeth's tormented guilty conscience is an important aspect of the social environment of this scene, and it could also be argued that it is has value as a part of play's political environment.

Beats

Beats are rhythmic units of action within the scene. Each unit has its own *tempo*, which derives from fluctuating levels of tension within the scene. A scene's *rhythm* is thus made up of the surging and receding tempi that result from fluctuating levels of tension or intensity that actors (and directors) bring to the scene. One could decide that the first beat of the sleepwalking scene starts at Lady Macbeth's entrance and ends at her first recognition that her hands are not getting clean. Subsequent beats might be marked off in terms of the escalation of her emotional intensity, and the scene could be said to climax with her despairing exit. Beats are an inextricable part of a play's overall rhythm. Mood, atmosphere, and tone are all affected by the manipulation of the rhythmic beats within each scene, and the correct breakdown of the play's dramatic action into beats is therefore one of the best ways of attracting and holding the audience's attention.

Objective

The objective is what the character *wants* or *needs* most, stated in the strongest, clearest possible terms. When choosing an objective for your character within a scene, try to specifically limit it to the immediate needs of the scene. The overall or larger objective for the entire play (which Stanislavski calls the "throughline of action") may be altogether different. Use only active, transitive verbs—that is, a *"doing of something to someone or something"*—for best results when choosing an objective. For example, Lady Macbeth's overall objective in *Macbeth* could be stated in the following way: "to make her husband King." However, her smaller, more immediate objective in the sleepwalking scene is "to rid herself of guilt" in the murder of Duncan. Choosing such moment-to-moment or scene-to-scene "mini" objectives makes the scene more potent, immediate, and playable for the actor. Note that each scene's objective ("to rid herself of guilt") is related but not identical to the throughline of action ("to make her husband King").

Action

The *action* refers to the specific strategy by which the character intends to *achieve the objective*. To continue with our example, in the sleepwalking scene, Lady Macbeth will achieve her *objective* ("to rid herself of guilt") through the *action* of washing imaginary blood from her hands. Choosing this action and linking it to this objective will put the actor's focus on the physical and psychological act of cleansing, which will contribute symbolic and emotional resonance to the scene, and give the actor something concrete to focus on in the moment. There may be multiple actions taken before an objective is achieved or only one. It is also possible that, no matter how many actions are taken, the objective is never achieved in the scene (such as in the scene used in our example). Note that the word *action* should not be confused with *activity*. Characters may pursue an action within a scene without moving a muscle; actions may be psychological, emotional, or physical.

Obstacles

Anything that blocks or prevents an action from achieving an objective is an obstacle. An obstacle may also be physical, emotional, or psychological. When an obstacle is encountered, a new action may be undertaken to continue to pursue the objective. For example, one could say that Lady Macbeth encounters an obstacle when she finds that she cannot wash the blood off her hands (therefore, she cannot achieve her objective of assuaging her guilt). This obstacle could be interpreted in two ways: as the result of her physical state (she is sleepwalking; therefore, she cannot see that her hands are in fact clean) or her psychological state (she is guilty; therefore, she will never be free of guilt). Either way, the obstacle causes her to attempt to achieve her objective (ridding herself of guilt) through new actions (such as berating her husband), but none of these new actions works either. In the face of this obstacle, Lady Macbeth finally gives up her objective and despairs that "all the perfumes of Arabia cannot sweeten this little hand."

Transitions

These are the moments that occur between the beats, linking one unit to the next. A transition is like a new inhalation in the "breathing" of the scene or like a pause in its rhythm. Frequently, transitions occur when the actor's relationship to the action or objective changes (e.g., the moment when he or she encounters an obstacle and must undertake a fresh action to achieve the objective would be a moment of transition).

Climax or Turning Point

The climax of the scene occurs at the moment of greatest tension, when emotions are highest and the actor's intensity is peaking. It marks a change: up until this time, the scene has been heading in one direction, and after it, a fresh direction is taken. It is important to identify the moment when your scene climaxes, as it has important implications for the build or shape the scene will ultimately take.

A student wrote the following sample character/scene analysis, based on the role of Lady Macbeth, for an introductory acting class. Look carefully at the choices this student has made in terms of decisions about where the beats lie, what the objectives are, and so on. Within these choices lies the skeleton of the student's interpretation as an actor. Note that a student director would follow the same breakdown but would also be responsible for determining motivations and actions for *all* characters in the scene, including the Gentlewoman and the Doctor. A scene analysis by a directing student would therefore not have such a detailed breakdown of one character's point of view, as we shall see in the following example by an acting student; yet the directing student would have to grapple with other kinds of questions, such as the scene's relation to the play as a whole, to its overarching themes and images, and, most important, how the scene fits into the overall rhythm of the play. However, the basic procedure is the same.

Student Sample Character/Scene Analysis

Melissa Newton

Lady Macbeth's Last Sleep

Shakespeare's Lady Macbeth is the highly political, social-climbing wife of an ambitious general in the Scottish army. Upon hearing of the witches' prophesy that he will one day be king, she takes sides with them, and convinces her husband to murder the current King, Duncan. She urges her husband to take action by mocking him and accusing him of cowardice. She is a spiritually evil character who is ultimately tormented by maddening visions of her deeds. Her disease, as the doctor says in this scene, is incurable, since she cannot repent. The sleepwalking scene from act 5, scene 1, reveals the turmoil of her inner thoughts and emotions, a side of her character that the audience otherwise only sees in snatches. We know from earlier in the play that she would be willing to dash out her baby's brains if it meant getting the crown for her husband; this woman is therefore (in my interpretation of the role) dangerous and perhaps even a bit unbalanced mentally. My analysis of the sleepwalking scene below reflects my interpretation of her as on the brink of madness.

Beats: The first beat of the scene begins with Lady Macbeth's entrance and ends on the line, "What, will these hands ne'er be clean?" The second beat begins with her next line, "No more o' that, my lord, no more o' that . . ." and the third beat begins on the line, "Wash your hands, put on your nightgown . . ."

Objectives: Lady Macbeth's objectives in this scene are:

1. (first beat) *to wash the blood (i.e., the guilt)* off her hands ("Out, damned spot; out, I say!")

2. (second beat) *to make her husband stop acting guilty* ("No more o' that, my lord, no more o' that: you mar all with this starting")

3. (third beat) *to hide their guilt* ("Wash your hands, put on your nightgown, look not so pale")

Actions and obstacles: Her actions are: to achieve objective 1) (to wash the blood off her hands), *she rubs her hands obsessively*. Obstacle: in her dream state, they will not become clean. To achieve objective 2) (to make her husband stop acting guilty), *she berates and taunts him* ("Fie, my lord, fie, a soldier, and afeard?") Obstacle : in her dream-state, he does not respond. To achieve objective 3) (to hide their guilt) *she runs away* ("To bed, to bed, to bed."). Obstacle: her guilt will follow her wherever she goes.

Transitions and turning point/climax: The scene's transitions occur between the beats, on the lines indicated as marking off the beats. In the first transition, Lady Macbeth realizes her hands will "ne'er be clean," and her disturbed mind then temporarily focuses on her husband's frailties. In the next transition, she again despairs of ever cleansing her hand/conscience: "all the perfumes of Arabia . . ." The next transition marks the point at which she goes back again to her preoccupation with her husband's behavior and appearance ("Wash your hands, put on your nightgown, look not so pale . . ."), and the climax comes at the end of the scene, with her realization that all of the above attempts at expunging herself of guilt are futile, and they must deal with the consequences of their murderous ambition: "What's done cannot be undone." Note: Lady Macbeth's actions never work; thus she never achieves her objectives. She is ultimately driven mad, and dies.

The opening paragraph, which describes Lady Macbeth as a "highly political, social-climbing wife of an ambitious Scottish general," demonstrates a grasp of the given circumstances. Although more could have been written about them, the writer manages to convey clear interpretive choices about the character and the scene without enumerating every single aspect of the given circumstances, which might weigh down the essay with too much detail. That research is best confined to the early stages of note taking and does not have to appear in its entirety within the body of the essay. The analysis breaks down the scene into sensible beats (although arguments could be made for choosing beats in other places in the scene), and the technical elements are logically linked together to create a good, solid underlying structure to the role (and scene). The interpretation is backed up by a sensible, well-thought-out analysis, and although one might not necessarily agree with the assertion that Lady Macbeth is finally driven mad (e.g., one might argue for evidence of her madness throughout the play, and not just in this one scene), this character/scene analysis constitutes a good foundation or "blueprint" for acting or directing the scene according to the interpretation laid out in the analysis.

Notice that the character/scene analysis employs a unique style to facilitate the practical work of the individual actor or director. It departs somewhat from a strictly traditional essay structure (i.e., a thesis statement, body paragraphs, and a concluding argument). Instead, it has a flexible organization, the only imperative of which is that it clearly and concisely reflect the relationship of the units in the scene to the whole of the scene (and, ultimately, to the whole of the play). Bullet points may be used instead of numbers, for example, or objectives and actions may be linked through the use of graphics rather than through narrative. In other words, the organization of the character/scene analysis can take different shapes as long as it is as clear and to the point as possible. The ultimate goal remains the same: to create a workable, lucid "blueprint" for your approach to the scene or role.

The character/scene analysis is a manifestation of the fundamentals, the "sweat and blood," of theatrical practice. Whether articulating an approach to acting a role or to directing a scene, the character/scene analysis helps both reader and writer describe the "nuts and bolts" of the process. John Barrymore, one of the great American actors of the twentieth century, once remarked, "One of my chief regrets during my years in the theatre is that I couldn't sit in the audience and watch me." Wanting to inhabit the experience from all sides at once, Barrymore's appreciation of theatre extended across the footlights to embrace the audience, the written play text, and the shared joy in the actual living moment of its unfolding. Writing about theatre means writing about experience. Whether considering it as a practice, a history, a text, or an event, writing about that experience will provide you with an active and engaging subject.

✔ A Checklist for Writing a Character/Scene Analysis

❑   Have you taken the given circumstances of the scene into account?

❑   Does the analysis make a good case for the overall interpretation of the scene? That is, does it break the scene down into beats or units, and are the objectives, actions, transitions, obstacles, and climax all linked logically into a compelling or convincing interpretation?

❑   Does the analysis provide a clear, concise, "actable" guide to the scene?

Glossary of Theatrical Terms and Concepts

A BRIEF INTRODUCTION

To write a convincing argument, you need to make fine distinctions, and to make fine distinctions, you need a good vocabulary. Like any discipline, theatre has its own vocabulary and terminology, which provide you with the tools you need to say exactly what you mean. Theatrical terms and conventions have been evolving in tandem with thousands of years of stagecraft, playwriting, criticism, and artistry in the theatre. Knowing these terms and conventions is a crucial step in asking the right questions about drama and performance, questions that will lead to clear, convincing writing. Engaging with this vocabulary in your essay will make your argument more effective by giving your ideas more precision, sophistication, and scope. Being able to discuss the different capabilities of the *proscenium* versus the *arena* stage, for example, or to refer to a play's *dramatic structure* not only adds finesse to your writing but also places your argument in the larger context of the history and traditions of theatre writing. This glossary provides brief definitions and explanations for the basic terms, topics, and conventions of theatre today. It is by no means exhaustive in its scope; rather, its intention is to serve as a basic reference for this guide.

Conventions are helpful because they contain within them familiar patterns of seeing and thinking about theatre. Even in departures from convention, the structure of the convention is still useful as the thing departed *from*. It is important to note that a strong tradition exists within the theatre that seeks specifically to break with and challenge existing conventions as a way to make new statements and create new theatrical images. Thus, departing from convention becomes a way to express individual points of view. Some styles are particularly invigorating simply because they are new and leave existing norms behind. On the other hand, many "new" approaches and techniques are simply old ones rediscovered and put to new uses. Recognizing the "old" within the new can be a good way to write about and analyze theatre. Nonetheless, being familiar with the basic conventions of theatre allows you to write about theatre with the knowledge and authority needed to convince readers of your point of view.

absurdism: A stylistic term referring to plays that deal with the ridiculous aspects of human existence in an unknowable universe; an antirealistic style featuring techniques that highlight the inability of humans to communicate or relate to one another meaningfully. Ionesco, Beckett, and Pinter are examples of playwrights who have been labeled absurdist.

arena stage: Also called "theatre in the round," this stage is an acting area (elevated, flat, or sometimes sunken) completely surrounded or encircled by the audience. The audience can see itself across the way, making it more useful for a presentational style of theatre rather than an illusionistic one since the audience is constantly reminded of its own presence.

character: The individuals that "people" the dramatist's tale. Characters reveal the play's dramatic action as they react to the play's "given circumstances," to the incidents in the story, and to one another. A character may be *primary* or *secondary*. *Primary characters* speak the bulk of the play's dialogue and perform most of its dramatic action; *secondary characters* serve to flesh out the world of the play.

climax: A component of a play's dramatic structure. In the climax, the problems that have evolved in the rising action will come to a head. At this point, the basic issues come out in the open: battles (both literal and figurative) may be fought, sentiments may be declared, and a turning point in the action is reached.

comedy: A play that ends happily in which the protagonist adjusts to the society of the onstage world, usually after a series of comic difficulties.

commedia dell'arte: A form of popular theatre begun in the mid-sixteenth century in Northern Italy, it is arguably famous for most brilliantly employing the stock characters and plots that are still in use to this day. This type of theatre used half masks, symbolic costumes, memorized scenarios (*scenari*, or loosely outlined, basic plot formations) and memorized tricks (*lazzi*, or comic moments such as slipping on a banana peel) to satirize basic human instincts such as lust, gluttony, and greed.

costume: Any attire worn by actors in the course of bringing their characters to life. The costume designer works in tandem with the director to literally "clothe" the theatrical concept behind the production.

denouement: A component of a play's dramatic structure, it marks the overall resolution to the play, which provides a kind of closure to the action. Traditionally during this phase, an old world order is restored or a new one is created. In a comedy, family or other societal units are rejoined in new configurations, frequently with a marriage or a dance of some kind, whereas in a tragedy there will conversely be a dissolution of some societal bond or world order.

dialogue: Composed of the verbal exchanges between characters. The dramatic action of the play is fueled largely by (or contained in) the play's dialogue.

dramatic action: The advancement of incidents through the clash of forces in the play. These forces are embodied in or illustrated by characters that move the play toward the conclusion. Do not confuse dramatic action with *activity*, which is what the actors physically do onstage. Activity is a tool that helps the characters *realize* the dramatic action, but it is not the same thing as the dramatic action.

dramatic form: This refers to the *internal*, textual conventions of drama. It includes plot, story, character, dialogue, dramatic action, dramatic structure, exposition, rising action, climax, denouement, stock plots, and stock characters.

dramatic structure: The overall composition of the plot, story, and character; the manner in which the incidents are arranged and organized by the playwright.

dramaturgy: The study of the art and craft of playwrighting composition and play production in all its composite parts and interrelationships. Dramaturgy is a discipline that supports and enhances the director's vision of the play by examining a play from many different perspectives. While it involves a concentration on the dramatic structure of the play, it also includes a broader exploration of such elements as the culture of the place and time in which the play was written, the time period it takes place in, the history of other productions of the play, and biographical details about the playwright, among other things.

environmental stage: This term refers to staging that takes place outside a traditional theatre in an environment that the director deems suitable to the piece. Developed mainly in the 1960s, these productions sometimes completely dissolve the barriers between audience space and actor space so that performers and spectators mingle together as the performance (or "event") takes shape.

epic theatre: An approach to writing and producing plays in which the play unfolds in discrete episodes and appeals less to the spectators' emotion than to their intellect. Used most famously by Bertolt Brecht.

exposition: A component of a play's dramatic structure. The introductory phase that explains the *given circumstances* of the play and provides the audience with crucial information to understand the play. *Given circumstances* refers to all those details that make up the world of the play, that is, the play's environment and the relationships between primary characters.

expressionism: A theatrical movement originating around 1910 in Germany in which "reality" was conceived as individual, subjective experience. Plays often unfolded from a singular point of view, often that of the protagonist. Objects and sets were often designed in terms of the personal emotions and concerns of the protagonist. It seeks to depart from the conventions of realistic staging practices by experimenting with symbol and form over realism and exposition.

feminism: An ideological movement that examines gender dynamics across social, political, cultural, and artistic contexts. "Feminist theatre" is a blanket term that includes playwrights, practitioners, and critics who look closely at the ways women are represented in theatre.

forestage proscenium stage: This stage combines a forestage (a playing space jutting out in front of the main acting area) with a traditional picture frame, bringing the actors in front of the frame but also preserving the capabilities of the proscenium to hide scene changes and/or enclose the framed part of the stage on three sides. Audiences sit in front of the stage since sitting to the sides will restrict their view of the part of the stage inside the "picture frame."

genre: The categories by which plays have been classified and grouped together according to similarities in their structure and their effect on the audience. Tragedy and comedy are the largest such categories, and each of them is further subdivided into various subcategories.

inferior awareness: The audience has an inferior awareness when they know *less* than the main characters onstage. This creates dramatic tension because the audience must wait to discover the truth.

lighting: Lighting affects audience perceptions, helps to create mood, and is a powerful device in the overall design of the stage picture. Lighting is a way to enhance the glamour and energy of the stage picture. Spectacular lighting effects can literally "wake up" an audience, whereas low lighting can create alternative moods and atmospheres.

makeup: Makeup design can be used to accentuate the actor's features so that they are visible to the audience or, on the contrary, to create a kind of *mask*, altering the actors features to achieve a particular effect.

monologue: Spoken by one character like a soliloquy, but it is more closely related to other literary forms, including laments and lyric verse. A monologue can be an extended piece in itself, such as in the work of monologist Spaulding Gray.

mood: The emotional effect created by specific scenes or moments onstage. Mood is informed not only by the way a scene is written but also by key production elements, such as lighting, acting, and sound. A production's overall tone is the accumulation of its many different moods.

motif: A recurrent thematic or design element in a play.

naturalism: A theatrical (and literary) style featuring realistic detail that attempts to apply scientific methods and detachment to the study of human beings. Nineteenth-century writers such as Emile Zola and August Strindberg believed that such a naturalistic approach could reveal the laws and forces governing basic human behavior.

open-thrust stage: This is the stage of Shakespeare, and it consists of a platform (it may or may not be raised—sometimes the audience's seats are raised instead) for the acting area, which juts out before a stage wall in the back. The audience surrounds the platform on three sides. This stage brings the actor out in front of the "frame" for a more three-dimensional theatrical experience, and, although it can be used for illusionistic theatre, it is more often associated with *presentational* theatre—theatre that acknowledges its own fictitious nature.

plot: The sequence of incidents that compose the dramatic action of the play as seen by the audience.

properties: There are two basic kinds of properties (or "props"): *hand properties* and *set properties*. *Hand properties* include anything the actors can touch, hold, or pick up. They are extremely important because actors express character through their handling of them. *Set properties* are too large to be hand properties (although occasionally a set property will briefly become a hand property, such as when two characters lift and move a table). Although they can sometimes be objects from nature or from imaginary realms, set properties are usually furniture. Like hand properties, they are "animated" by the actor's use of them. *Set changes* (the moments between scenes in which set properties, lighting, and scenery may be changed) are an important influence on the rhythm and tempo of the overall performance.

proscenium stage: This is the classic "picture frame" stage, in which a frame is placed around the playing space (traditionally a curtain is lowered and raised in front of this space to signal the beginning and end of the performance) and the audience sits in front of it. The proscenium stage is now associated mainly with *illusionistic* theatre—theatre that presents the illusion that what is being watched is real life. The *box set* is a type of setting often associated with illusionism, in which the stage is enclosed on three sides and the audience sits where the fourth side (also known as the fourth wall) should be.

raked stage: A stage that tilts upward toward the back wall, thus increasing the visibility of figures placed in the back of the stage (the "upstage" area). As mentioned before, an actor walking upstage was literally walking uphill and vice versa. (See chapter 2 for a more detailed discussion of conventional ways to designate stage areas.)

realism: A stylistic term for plays that depict life onstage (often everyday life) in an especially realistic way. Realistic situations, settings, props, and costumes characterize these plays, which originated in Europe in the mid-nineteenth century. Closely associated with naturalism.

rising action: A component of a play's dramatic structure, it is the period during which complications develop. During this phase, the situation that was set forth in the exposition is complicated somehow; problems evolve, schemes are hatched, and in general the plot is "thickened."

scenery: This includes anything that alters the stage picture. There are three basic kinds of scenery: architectural (movable elements such as steps and doors), painted (such as flats and drops), and electronically projected (such as photographic slides and videos that are projected onto the upstage [back] wall or other onstage areas).

soliloquy: Spoken by one character, often when he or she is lost in thought, as in Hamlet's famous soliloquy beginning, "To be or not to be."

sound: Sound design includes any music before, during, and after a performance and any sound effects that occur during it. Music is obviously an expressive medium that can be used to enhance mood, rhythm, and emotion in a production. The basic function of sound design is to excite or enhance the imagination of the audience.

stagecraft: A term encompassing all the diverse practical arts that contribute to the theatrical production.

stock characters/plots: These are conventional figures and tales that are widely recognizable because of their constant appearance in various guises in drama throughout the world (and throughout history). Some of these forms took shape in medieval drama, but the Italian commedia dell'arte is perhaps most notable for the use and popularizing of stock characters and plots. Examples of stock characters include a young couple in love, a lustful old father, a foolish doctor, and a tricky servant. An example of a stock plot is two young lovers who wish to marry but meet the resistance of the young man's lustful old father, who wishes to marry the girl himself.

story: The incidents and conflicts that compose the play, including the previous (sometimes called precipitating) action, which is the thing that happened before the play begins to set the incidents in motion. The story includes those incidents and/or characters that do not appear onstage but that are nonetheless part of the story. All stories have a beginning, a middle, and an end, although it is possible for a play's story to be "circular" or to have other variations in its structure.

style: Describes visual, design, acting, and writing approaches and the particular manner of expression that the playwright uses. Style can be classified in many different ways, such as by the time period, author, genre (such as tragedy or comedy), or movement (realism, absurdism, and so on) employed.

superior awareness: The audience possesses a superior awareness when they know *more* about what is going on than most of the characters inhabiting the onstage world. This creates dramatic tension because the audience will wonder when, how, or if the main characters will discover the truth that they already know.

suspension of disbelief: A term developed by English romantic poet Samuel Taylor Coleridge that describes the ideal mental and emotional state the audience inhabits when watching a play. They willingly set aside expectations for truth and reality as a way of enjoying the illusion of the play. This convention is naturally associated with illusionistic theatre practices, such as the proscenium stage, which encourage the audience to regard the play as a "slice of real life."

theatrical conventions: The recognizable structures of and/or approaches to theatre, the "common language" of the discipline.

They can be physical or theoretical and can include such diverse components as theatre buildings, properties, scenery, criticism, and styles of directing or acting.

theatrical effect: An element of a play or production (including but not limited to design elements, acting styles, dialogue, and so on) that conveys meaning to the reader or audience.

theme: An implicit or recurrent idea or image that conveys an important part of the play's overall artistic, emotional, or intellectual content.

tone: The overall effect of all the appropriate moods in a production; the tone contains the director's total interpretation of the play's message or idea.

tragedy: A play in which the protagonist undergoes a tragic or deeply unhappy experience, often but not always involving death.

tragicomedy: A play that combines tragic and comic elements to create unsettling or ambiguous theatrical effect.

well-made play: A formulaic approach to playwrighting that originated with French playwright Eugene Scribe (1791–1861), who perfected the skillful crafting of a play to arouse suspense in the spectator. It is characterized by a consistent dramatic structure that was (and continues to be) a model, or "formula," for generations of playwrights. It includes a careful exposition; a suspenseful, "cause-and-effect" arrangement of incidents; rising action that builds to a climax; and the revelation of key information that has been withheld from the audience.

Works Cited

Aristophanes. "The Clouds." In *Four Plays by Aristophanes*. New York: Penguin Books, 1962.

Barranger, Milly. *Theatre: A Way of Seeing*. New York: Wadsworth, 2005.

Becket, Samuel. *Waiting for Godot: A Tragicomedy in Two Acts*. New York: Grove Press, 1994.

Bevington, David. *The Complete Works of Shakespeare*. New York: Longman, 2003.

Brook, Peter. *The Empty Space*. New York: Avon Books, 1968.

Carlson, Marvin. "Andrea Breth's Hedda Gabler." In *Western European Stages*. Vol. 7. New York: Graduate Center of the City University of New York, 1995–1996, 61–62.

Chekhov, Anton. *The Three Sisters*. Kila, Mont.: Kessinger Publishers, 2004.

Chinoy, Helen, and Toby Cole. *Directors on Directing*. New York: Allyn & Bacon, 1963.

Churchill, Caryl. *Cloud 9*. New York: Theatre Communications Group, 1995.

Fornes, Maria Irene. *Fefu and Her Friends*. New York: PAJ Publications, 1978.

Ibsen, Henrik. *A Doll's House*. Lenox, Mass.: Hard Press, 2006.

Johnson, S. F. "Introduction to *Julius Caesar*." In *William Shakespeare: The Complete Works*. Edited by Alfred Harbage. Baltimore: Penguin Books, 1969.

Miller, Arthur. *Death of a Salesman*. New York: Penguin Books, 1998.

————. "Tragedy and the Common Man." In *Types of Drama: Plays and Essays*. Edited by Sylvan Barnet et al. Glenview, Ill.: Scott, Foresman and Company, 1989.

Nagler, A. M. *A Source Book in Theatrical History*. New York: Dover Books, 1959.

Norman, Marsha. *'Night, Mother*. New York: Hill and Wang, 1983.

O'Neill, Eugene. *Long Day's Journey into Night*. New Haven, Conn.: Yale University Press, 2002.

Ridley, Clifford. "Stoppard's 'Invention of Love' at Wilma." *Philadelphia Inquirer*, 18 February 2000, W35.

Shakespeare, William. *Henry V*. In *The Complete Works of Shakespeare*. Edited by David Bevington. New York: Longman, 2003.

————. *Julius Caesar*. In *The Complete Works of Shakespeare*. Edited by David Bevington. New York: Longman, 2003.

————. *Macbeth*. In *The Complete Works of Shakespeare*. Edited by David Bevington. New York: Longman, 2003.

————. *A Midsummer Night's Dream*. In *The Complete Works of Shakespeare*. Edited by David Bevington. New York: Longman, 2003.

————. *Othello*. In *The Complete Works of Shakespeare*. Edited by David Bevington. New York: Longman, 2003.

————. *Romeo and Juliet*. In *The Complete Works of Shakespeare*. Edited by David Bevington. New York: Longman, 2003.

Stoppard, Tom. *The Invention of Love*. New York: Grove Press, 1997.

————. *Voyage*. London: Faber and Faber, 2002.

Taylor, John Russel. *The Rise and Fall of the Well-Made Play*. New York: Hill and Wang, 1967.

Tynan, Kenneth. "Olivier's Othello." In *Olivier at Work*. Edited by Lyn Haill. London: Nick Hern Books, 1989.

Wilde, Oscar. *The Importance of Being Earnest*. New York: Penguin Classics, 2001.

Wilder, Thornton. *Our Town*. New York: Harper, 1960.

Williams, Tennessee. *The Glass Menagerie*. New York: New Directions Publishing Corporation, 1999.

Index

Questions to Ask Yourself When Revising Your Writing

1. Have I completely understood what I have done, read, or been told?

2. Are my notes accurate, and do they distinguish between my thoughts and words and those of the author(s)?

3. Does my opening paragraph prepare the reader for all that follows?

4. Does my writing flow smoothly and logically from point to point? Are there adequate transitions between sentences and paragraphs?

5. Does each sentence make its case completely, concisely, and unambiguously?

6. Is every fact or opinion supported with a reference, example, or explanation?

7. Have I proofread and revised for spelling, grammatical, and typographical errors? Have I really said what I intended to say?

8. Are my graphs equipped with clearly labeled axes (including units) and sufficiently detailed explanatory captions? Are my tables equipped with suitable column headings (including units) and captions? Are my figures and tables largely self-sufficient?

9. Are all numbers followed by appropriate units of measurement?

10. Does the title of my paper or report reflect its specific content?